T0158857

Inspired by the book *This Is Who We Are How We Become The Sons Of God* written by Beth Bonner

THE SHUNAMMITE WOMAN

THIS IS WHO WE ARE; BECOMING THE SONS OF GOD

JANE VAN LAAR

WestBow
PRESS®
A DIVISION OF THOMAS NELSON
& ZONDERVAN

Copyright © 2017 Jane van Laar.

All rights reserved. No part of this book may be used or reproduced by any means, graphic, electronic, or mechanical, including photocopying, recording, taping or by any information storage retrieval system without the written permission of the author except in the case of brief quotations embodied in critical articles and reviews.

Scripture taken from the New King James Version. Copyright © 1979, 1980, 1982 by Thomas Nelson, Inc. Used by permission. All rights reserved.

Image credit: Jane van Laar

WestBow Press books may be ordered through booksellers or by contacting:

WestBow Press
A Division of Thomas Nelson & Zondervan
1663 Liberty Drive
Bloomington, IN 47403
www.westbowpress.com
1 (866) 928-1240

Because of the dynamic nature of the Internet, any web addresses or links contained in this book may have changed since publication and may no longer be valid. The views expressed in this work are solely those of the author and do not necessarily reflect the views of the publisher, and the publisher hereby disclaims any responsibility for them.

ISBN: 978-1-5127-7427-6 (sc)
ISBN: 978-1-5127-7428-3 (e)

Library of Congress Control Number: 2017901808

Print information available on the last page.

WestBow Press rev. date: 10/20/2017

The Shunammite Woman

Contents

The Shunnamite Woman	2 Kings 4:8-37	1
The Shunammite Woman	Week 1 Day 1	3
Her Characteristics	Week 1 Day 2	7
Her Characteristics	Week 1 Day 3	10
Her Characteristics	Week 1 Day 4	13
Her Characteristics	Week 1 Day 5	18
This is who we are		23
Elisha	Week 2 Day 1	24
Elijah	Week 2 Day 2	31
Elijah Ascends To Heaven	Week 2 Day 3	36
Elisha Begins His Miracles	Week 2 Day 4	44
Elijah, Elisha and The Shunammite Woman	Week 2 Day 5	49
God's Plan For You		54
The Upper Room	Week 3 Day 1	57
The Bed	Week 3 Day 2	62
The Bed	Week 3 Day 3	66
The Bed	Week 3 Day 4	71
What a Beautiful Bed	Week 3 Day 5	75
The Table	Week 4 Day 1	80
The Table	Week 4 Day 2	87
The Table Your Desk/Your Notebook	Week 4 Day 3	92
The Table	Week 4 Day 4	98
The Table	Week 4 Day 5	102
God Revealed		105
The Chair	Week 5 Day 1	107

The Chair	Week 5 Day 2	111
The Chair God sits	Week 5 Day 3	114
The Chair- Judgement Seat of Christ	Week 5 Day 4	123
The Chair	Week 5 Day 5	127
The Shunammite Woman		133
The Lampstand	Week 6 Day 1	135
The Lampstand	Week 6 Day 2	142
The Lampstand and The Light	Week 6 Day 3	148
The Lampstand and The Light	Week 6 Day 4	151
The Lampstand	Week 6 Day 5	156
This Is Who You Are		161
Reference Page		163
Thank You		164

The Shunammite Woman   Painting by Jane van Laar

My God blesses me with words. He gives me words and shows me scripture. I write what I hear Him say. I am not a strong writer. I am not a bible scholar but I have heard Him direct me to scripture and He has placed before me others who gave me words of inspiration. I praise His name for His guidance and assurance as He has given me what I have presented to you.

I pray your blessings overflow.

Jane van Laar

Email me with comments:janevanlaar@yahoo.com

The Shunnamite Woman

2 Kings 4:8-37

"Now it happened one day that Elisha went to Shunem, where there was a notable woman, and she persuaded him to eat some food. So it was, as often as he passed by, he would turn in there to eat some food. And she said to her husband, "Look now, I know that this is a holy man of God, who passes by us regularly. Please let us make a small upper room on the wall; and let us put a bed for him there, and a table and a chair and a lampstand; so it will be, whenever he comes to us, he can turn in there." And it happened one day that he came there, and he turned in to the the upper room and lay down there. Then he said to Gehazi his servant, "Call this Shunammite woman." When he had called her, she stood before him. And he said to him, "Say now to her, 'Look, you have been concerned for us with all this care. What can I do for you? Do you want me to speak on your behalf to the king or to the commander of the army?" She answered, "I dwell among my own people." So he said,"What then is to be done for her?" And Gehazi answered, "Actually she has no son, and her husband is old." So he said, "Call her." When he had called her, she stood in the doorway. Then he said, "About this time next year you shall embrace a son." And she said, "No, my lord, man of God, do not lie to your maid servant!" But the woman conceived, and bore a son when the appointed time had come, of which Elisha had told her. And the child grew. Now it happened one day that he went out to his father, to the reapers. And he said to his father, "My head, my head!" So he said to a servant, "Carry him to his mother." When he had taken him and brought him to his mother, he sat on her knees till noon, and then died. And she went up and laid him on the bed of the man of God, shut the door upon him, and went out. Then she called to her husband, and said, "Please send me one of the young men and one of the donkeys, that I may run to the man of God and come back." So he said,"Why are you going to him today? It is neither the New Moon nor the Sabbath." And she said,"It is well." Then she saddled a donkey, and said to her servant, "Drive, and go forward; do not slacken the pace for me unless I tell you." And so she departed, and went to the man of God at Mount Carmel. So it was, when the man of God saw her afar off, that he said to his servant, Gehazi, "Look, the Shunammite woman! Please run now to meet her, and say to her, 'Is it well with you? Is it well with your husband? Is it well with the child?" And she answered, "It is well." Now when she came to the man of God at the hill, she caught him by the feet, but Gehazi came near to her to push her away. But the man of God said, "Let her alone; for her soul is in deep distress, and the Lord has hidden it from me, and has not told me" So she said, "Did I ask a son of my lord? Did I not say, 'Do not deceive me?" Then he said to Gehazi, "Get yourself ready, and take my staff in your hand, and be on your way. If you meet anyone, do not greet him; and if anyone greets you, do not answer him: but lay my staff on the face of the child." And the mother of the child said, "As the Lord lives, and as your soul lives, I will not leave you." So he arose and followed her. Now Gehazi went on ahead of them, and laid the staff on the face of the child; but there was neither voice nor hearing. Therefore he went back to meet him, and told him, saying, "The child has not awakened." When Elisha came into the house, there was the child, lying dead on his bed. He went in therefore, shut the door behind the two of them, and prayed to the Lord. And he went up and lay on the child, and put his mouth on his mouth, his eyes on his eyes, and his hands on his hands; and he stretched himself out on the child, and the flesh of the child became warm. He returned and walked back and forth in the house, and again went up and stretched himself out on him; then the child sneezed seven times and the child opened his eyes. And he called Gehazi and said, "Call this Shunammite woman." So he called her. And when she came into him, he said. "Pick up your son." So she went in, fell at his feet, and bowed to the ground; then she picked up her son and went out."

The Shunammite Woman

WEEK 1 DAY 1

The Shunammite Woman is based on 2 Kings 4:8-37. This scripture, along with Beth Bonner's book, **This Is Who We Are - How We Become The Sons of God** is the basis for our study.

Beth writes: "What is our purpose? Are we here simply to breath in and out? Or is there more? Join me as I explore the possibility that we are at the center of the creative force of life and as a result, we have a responsibility to not only do the right thing for this planet, but also be the becoming of the 'Sons of God.'"

Read: 2 Kings 4:8-37

The Shunammite woman was from Shunem. Her city is her first characteristic. We are given no name for her or even any indication of a name. So she will only be referred to as "the Shunammite woman". I wish I knew her name and I am sure she does have a name. A person referred to from their country or land is representative of that land. Three other women in the bible are from Shunem. Only one is stated by name.

The first characteristic of our study is the land she is from_____(1)
In the scriptures below underline Shunem.

Joshua tells us about her land in the scripture, as we see Jacob divide the land among his twelve sons. This land is one of the portions of Israel:

"The fourth lot came out to Issachar, for the children of Issachar according to their families. And their territory went to Jezreel, and included Chesulloth, Shunem,... their border ended at the Jordan: sixteen cities with their villages. This was the inheritance of the tribe of the children of Issachar according to their families, the cities and their villages."   Joshua 19:17,18 & 23.

You can see this land is off the coast of the Mediterranean Sea on the east side of the northern part of the Jordan River. Look in your Bible at a Map of the times.

Refer to Genesis 30:17, 18

"And God listened to Leah, and she conceived and bore Jacob a fifth son. Leah said, 'God has given me my wages, because I have given my maid to my husband.' So she called his name Issachar."

Who was Issachar?_____(2)

In Genesis 49, Jacob speaks his last words to his sons. Issachar is blessed by Jacob in verses 14 and 15.

"Issachar is a strong donkey, lying down between two burdens; He saw that rest was good, and that the land was pleasant: He bowed his shoulder to bear a burden and became a band of slaves." Genesis 49:14 and 15

Jacob's words to Issachar speaks of____ (3) burdens. Between the two burdens are the time of plenty after the flood and famine. Jacob's words portend a heavy enslavement following a time of plenty. The time of plenty is the time following Noah's return to the land after the flood in Genesis.(2)

"So God blessed Noah and his sons and said to them, 'Be fruitful and multiply, and fill the earth.'" Genesis 9:1

The "shoulder of burden to bear" is from his birth. Refer back up to why Leah named him Issachar. "God has given me my wages, because I have given my maidservant to my husband."

The burden to bear was _____(4)

Can you see the two burdens to bear?

What is your heavy enslavement?
What is your land of plenty?

Obviously, the Shunammite woman was caring.

David experienced this same care by another Shunammite woman. "So they sought for a lovely young woman throughout all the territory of Israel, and found Abishag the Shunammite, and brought her to the king. The young woman was very lovely; and she cared for the king, and she served him; but the king did not know her." 1 Kings 1:3-4

This search for a lovely young woman would be equal to our Miss America. I guess Donald Trump is the king. David is about 70 years old when he chooses his Ms. Shunem. The search was the territory of Israel. The care she gave was a nurse maid. Galen, the second century Greek physician, and the Jewish historian, Josephus, noted that using a healthy person's body warmth to care for a sick person is a medical procedure. (NKJV Study Bible, pg. 518)

Abishag is also mentioned in 1 Kings 1:15 where she met Bathsheba while caring for David.

Look at Song of Solomon. It is the_____ **(5)**, who is the bride of Solomon, his queen. Shunammite is not a name but a title. She is thought to be from Shunem. Remember that Solomon is David's son.

These three Shunammite women, the one we study, Solomon's queen and Abishag, were caring and giving. That is who they were. **Does that speak of the quality of the people of the land of Shunem?**

God blessed these women. Many of God's caring and giving women are blessed. Look at the below scripture and record who or what God blessed and how:

Genesis 1:22
Who?
How?

Genesis 2:3
What?
How?

Genesis 9:1
Who?
How?

Genesis 12:2-3
Who?
How?

"I will make you a great nation; I will bless you and make your name great; and you shall be a blessing. I will bless those who bless you, and I will curse him who curses you: and in all the families of the earth shall be blessed." Genesis 12:2-3

These were blessed from the beginning in Genesis.

The word blessed expresses the idea of God's smile. Don't you love to think of God smiling on YOU? He does!!

Blessed also means the warmth of His pleasure.

Where has God blessed you?

Pray today thanking God for His blessings to you. Watch Him smile.

Answers:

1. **Shunem**
2. **Fifth son of Leah and Jacob**
3. **Two**
4. **Leah and sin**
5. **Shunammite**

Who: Adam and Eve
How:"Be fruitful and multiply and fill the earth and subdue it; have dominion over the fish of the sea, over the birds of the air, and over every living thing that moves of the earth."

What: The seventh day
How: With rest from all His work

Who: Noah and his son's
How: Be fruitful and multiply and fill the earth

Who: Abram
How: Listed above from the scripture.

Her Characteristics

WEEK 1 DAY 2

Today we continue our study with the characteristics of the Shunammite Woman. I wanted to name her, but all my names were inappropriate-- "Shu" or "Mite" or "Am" would work because we are studying her to become who we are.

Why do you think that she was not specifically named?

On day 1, we studied one of her characteristics. **She was from_____(1)**

Shumen, where she lived, was part of Issachar's lot from Jacob. Issachar is one of the son's of Jacob, a Hebrew. Therefore Issacher is one of the twelve tribes of Jacob. The Shunammite woman is a Hebrew, she is Jewish.

Look at 2 Kings 4:23: **How does the husband respond to her request "that I may run to the man of God and come back?"(2)**

Read in Exodus 20 about the Jewish law concerning the Sabbath: "Six days you shall labor and do all your work, but the seventh day is the Sabbath of the Lord your God. In it you shall do no work: you nor your son, nor your daughter, nor your male or female servant, nor your cattle, nor your stranger who is within your gates. For in six days the Lord made the heavens and the earth, the sea and all that is in them, and rested the seventh day. Therefore the Lord blessed the Sabbath day and hallowed it."

SABBATH means_____(3) . Her husband was working, so it was not the Sabbath. Her son and all the servants were also in the field.

"When will the New Moon be past, that we may sell grain?" Amos 8:5

NEW MOON was the first day of the month on the Hebrew calendar, a day of special sacrifices, a feast day, and a Sabbath day.

The Shunammite woman was a Jewish woman from all the evidence above.
Where were you born and raised?
Where you are from is a characteristic of "Who you are."

The third characteristic is that she is notable. This Shunammite woman was worthy of note, distinguished and prominent. One definition for notable is efficient or capable in performance of housewifely duties.

How would you define her as notable?

Here are some synonyms of notable: Bright, distinguished, illustrious, luminous, noble, eminent, noteworthy, outstanding, prominent, prestigious, redoubtable, star, and superior.

Now that you have gotten to know her for the past few days, which word/ words describe your vision of her more?

The NKJV Bible says that the word notable's literal meaning is Great! My choice is noble. Mostly because when I quickly read the scripture the first time I saw noble instead of notable. So, I was happy to see noble in the synonyms. Look at Philippians for some familiar words about noble:

"Finally, brethren, whatever things are true, whatever things are noble, whatever things are just, whatever things are pure, whatever things are lovely, whatever things are of good report, if there is any virtue and if there is anything praiseworthy---meditate on these things." Phil 4:8

Noble – describes that which is of honorable character.
Which word describes you?
Which word would others use to describe you?
Are the words above "who you are"?

Her fourth characteristics is that she was married. **How is the husband further described in 2 Kings 4:14?** _____(4)

In 2 Kings 4:9&10, she speaks to her husband about the upper room. **Her first words in verse 9 are ?**_____(5)

What are the words that you use to get your husbands attention?

In verse 10, she uses the word_____ (6). **Who are you when you speak to the significant people in your life? Do you honor them with please and thank you, with kindness?**

If this is an area of your life that you need to improve, take the time now to write a prayer asking God to help you be more patient and kind to others around you.

End your prayer with these words from Phil.4:8.
"Finally, brethren, whatever things are true, whatever things are noble, whatever things are just, whatever things are pure, whatever things are lovely, whatever things are of good report, if there is any virtue and if there is anything praiseworthy–meditate on these things." Phil 4:8

ANSWERS:

1. Shunem
2. Why are you going to him today? It is neither the New Moon nor the Sabbath.
3. Rest
4. Old
5. Look Now
6. Please

Her Characteristics

WEEK 1 DAY 3

We have studied these characteristics of the Shunnamite woman:

1.

2.

3.

4.

Let's look at her fifth characteristic. "I dwell among my people." 2 Kings 4:13 She was a dweller.

Read Acts 7:29 "Then, at this saying, Moses fled and became a dweller in the land of Midian, where he had two sons." **Who dwelled in the land of Midian?** _____(5)

"I will dwell in the house of the Lord Forever ." **This scripture is?**_____(6)

By her words we see that she was content in her situation. She was childless so she dwelled with all the others in her city. **From 2 Kings 4:8-12, how do you think she dwelt?**

Can you relate to her?

Are you childless or an empty nester?

How do you spend your time in service to others?

Numbers 23:9 speaks of the Israelites when Balaam looks down on them to curse them. "There! A people dwelling alone, not reckoning itself among the nations." From the worship site of pagan idolatry, Balaam viewed Israel from a distance and saw that they were a people distinct from all other nations. (NKJV Study Bible pg. 249)

Can someone look at your love for Christ and make you distinct from the world?

"By faith, Abraham dwelt in the land of promise as in a foreign country, dwelling in tents with Isaac and Jacob, the heirs with him of the same promise;" Hebrews 11:9 Abraham did not know where he was going, yet he still placed his trust in God.   Abram and Sarai name is changed by God to Abraham and Sarah. Faith means obediently stepping into the unknown. Abraham did this, and God considered him righteous because of it.

Underline the word **righteousness** below:
"And Abram believed in the Lord, and God accounted it to Abram for his righteousness." Gen. 15:6

"What then shall we say that Abraham our father has found according to the flesh? For if Abraham was justified by works, he was something to boast about, but not before God, and it was accounted to him for righteousness." Now to him who works, the wages are not counted as grace but as debt. But to him who does not work but believes on Him who justifies the ungodly, his faith is accounted for righteousness, just as David also describes the blessedness of the man to whom God imputes righteousness apart from works: Blessed are those whose lawless deeds are forgiven, and whose sins are covered; blessed is the man to whom the Lord shall not impute sin." Does this blessedness then come upon the circumcised only, or upon the uncircumcised also? For we say that faith was accounted to Abraham for righteousness. How then was it accounted? While he was circumcised or uncircumcised? Not while circumcised but while uncircumcised. And he received the sign of circumcision, a seal of the righteousness of the faith which he had while still uncircumcised, that righteousness might be imputed to them also, and the father of circumcision to those who not only are of the circumcision, but who also walk in the steps of the faith which our father Abraham had while still uncircumcised.." Romans 4:1-12

God made a promise to Abram. **Abram BELIEVED!**

God commanded Abram. **Abram OBEYED!**

Abram and Sarai are notable for their **BELIEF** and **OBEDIENCE** to God.

It is this belief, faith in the living God, that saves the sinner from sin. Old Testament times were characterized by faith in the living God, not good deeds. Abram was saved because he believed in God not by his righteous living but so being declared righteous by God.

The only valid work is the work of faith. "Then they said to Him, 'What shall we do, that we may work the works of God?' Jesus answered and said to them, 'This is the work of God, that you **believe** in Him whom He sent.'" John 6:28,29

How do you see the Shunamite Woman as faithful to God?

In order to dwell where God wants you to be today, do you need to step out in faith?

Are their areas of your life that you need to remember that you are part of the Kingdom of God and you need to faithfully give your all to Him? What are these areas?

Corrie ten Boom used these words to speak to people in deep depression, in loneliness or in prison as she witnessed to others after her time in prison during the Holocaust: "There is no pit so deep, that God's love is not deeper still."

Those words have touched my soul when times had no hope. God is always deeper than our troubles. The well is deep rooted, go deeper – dwell – but God is still with us. God is with us in the deeper, deepest of deep.

End with a prayer for the Lord to strengthen your faith remembering the strong faith of love ones who are and were faithful.

ANSWERS:

1. **Shunem**
2. **Jewish**
3. **Notable**
4. **Married–old man**
5. **Moses**
6. **Ps.23**

Her Characteristics

WEEK 1 DAY 4

Scripture Reference:2 Kings 4:8-12.Today we look at four other characteristics. So far, we have seen these:

1.

2.

3.

4.

5.

The sixth characteristic of the Shunammite woman is that she was a maidservant.

"And she said, 'No my lord, Man of God, do not lie to your maidservant!'" 2 Kings 4:16

She describes herself as maidservant.

"Boaz asked Ruth, 'Who Are You?' So she answered, 'I am Ruth, your maidservant. Take your maidservant under your wing, for you are a close relative.'" Ruth 3:9

What does Boaz ask her?(6)

Ruth had previously called herself a foreigner. A foreigner was a person whose loyalty belongs to someone else. Ruth now uses the word maidservant, which is the opposite to foreigner. Maidservant is the feminine form of bondservant.

"Paul, a bondservant of Jesus Christ, called to be an apostle..." Romans 1:1

Who is calling himself a bondservant of Jesus Christ in this scripture?
_____(7) Paul is speaking to the Roman Empire. The Romans are only aware

of forced slavery. But Paul speaks of the voluntary slavery in Exodus. The word servant and the laws are different. Voluntary slavery is slavery out of love. See Paul's reference below.

"Now these are the judgements which you shall set before them: If you buy a Hebrew servant, he shall serve six years; and in the seventh, he shall go free and pay nothing. If he comes in by himself, he shall go out by himself, if he comes in married, then his wife shall go out with him. If his master has given him a wife, and she has borne him sons or daughters, the wife and her children shall be her master's, and he shall go out by himself. But if the servant plainly says, 'I love my master, my wife, and my children: I will not go out free', then his master shall bring him to the judges. He shall also bring him to the door, or to the doorpost, and his master shall pierce his ear with an awl; and he shall serve him forever." Exodus 21:1-6

The last few verses cover the servant who stays a slave to his master. What are these words?_____**(8)**

How are the words spoken?_____**(9)**

Paul uses the word 'bondservant' to show his voluntary love to his Master, Jesus Christ. He plainly describes that his service is to the Lord. He states his love for Jesus.

Peter uses the word maidservant in Acts 2:17-18 when he repeats the words of the prophet Joel.

"And it shall come to pass in the last days, says God, that I will pour out of My Spirit on all flesh; your sons and daughters shall prophesy, your young men shall see visions, your old men shall dream dreams, and **My** menservants and **My** maidservants I will pour out My Spirit in those days." Joel 2:28-32

What is the word prior to menservants and maidservants?_____**(10) Who is MY?**_____**(11) Who is pouring out the Spirit?**_____**(12) Who then are the menservants and maidservants?**_____**(13)**

"Then Mary said, 'Behold the maidservant of the Lord! Let it be to me according to your word.'" Luke 1:38 "For He has regarded the lowly state of His maidservant; Luke 1:48

Who is speaking?_____**14)**

And to whom does she speak?_____(15)

What is Mary saying to the angel?_____(16)

Maidservant suggests humility before the Lord and a readiness for faithful and obedient service which should characterize every believer. (NKJV Study Bible pg. 1592)

Looking back on the words of the Shunammite woman, what were the words she used concerning maidservant? "Do not lie to your maidservant"

She was afraid he was lying about what?_____(17)

In your own words, why does she refer to herself as a maidservant?

The seventh characteristic is that the Shunammite woman is childless when we first meet her.

"And Gehazi answered, 'Actually, she has no son, and her husband is old.'" 2 Kings 4:14

What is your first thought when you read this verse?

Had the upper room been set for Elisha before or after these words?___(18)

Did the Shunammite woman serve in the place that she dwelled more after or before the prophet blessed her with a child?_____(19)

If you are childless for whatever reason including that your children are out of the home, your service to the Lord should not be any different. Serve as the Lord instructs.

"About this time next year you shall embrace a son." 2 Kings 4:16

What does Elisha promise her?_____(20)
Notice, not only a child, but a son. Did the Shunammite woman ask for a son"?_____(21)

"So she said, 'Did I ask a son of my lord?'" 2 Kings 4:28–29

What is her response in 2 Kings 4:16?_____(22)

After years of frustration, the Shunammite woman felt that even Elisha, a man of God, could not fulfill such a promise. **Who are others in the Bible that waited a long time for a promised child?**_____(23)

The next verse is in the next season of which Elisha has made his promise to her. "But the woman conceived, and bore a son when the appointed time had come, of which Elisha had told her." 2 Kings 2:17

This birth is similar to the fulfillment of a promise of God. Read Gen.21. Name some similarities:_____(25)

Hebrews 11:12 describes Abraham "as good as dead." What a miracle to Abraham. What a miracle to the Shunammite woman's husband. I am sure that she thought her husband "as good as dead" also.

God provides even when our thoughts are as "good as dead."

What areas of life have you given up and see no hope?

Let your prayer be today in God's hope. God's journey for you is hopeful. Put your faith in God's promise to you. Pray and read Jeremiah 29:11 "For I know the thoughts I think toward you, says the Lord, thoughts of peace and not of evil, to give you a future and a hope."

ANSWERS:

1. From Shumen
2. Jewish
3. Notable
4. Married to old man
5. Dweller

6. Who are you
7. Paul
8. I love my master and my children. I will not go out free
9. The words are spoken plainly
10. My maidservant/My bondservant
11. God
12. God
13. People who are bonded to God; people who are part of God's Kingdom
14. May
15. Angel – Gabriel
16. (your answer)
17. The gift of a child
18. Before
19. No different
20. A son
21. No
22. And she said, "No my lord, Man of God."
23. Abraham and Sarah
24. Sarah & Abraham are both old. Isaac was a promise of God

Her Characteristics

WEEK 1 DAY 5

Today we look at the last two characteristics of the Shunammite woman. So far we have seen these characteristics:

1. From Shumen
2. A Jewish woman
3. Notable
4. Dweller
5. Married (to an old man)
6. Maidservant
7. Childless – then blessed with a son

Let's continue to look at the Shunammite woman's characteristics:

The eighth characteristic is that she was in deep distress.

"And the child grew. Now it happened one day that he went out to his father, to the reapers. (19) And he said to his father, 'My head, my head!' So he said to a servant, 'Carry him to his mother.' (20) When he had taken him and brought him to his mother, he sat on her knees till noon, and then died. (21) And she went up and laid him on the bed of the man of God, shut the door upon him, and went out. (22)then she called to her husband, and said. 'Please send me one of the donkeys, that I may run to the man of God and come back.' (23) so he said, 'Why are you going to him today? It is neither the New Moon nor the Sabbath.' And she said, 'It is well.' (24) Then she saddled a donkey, and said to her servant, 'Drive, and go forward; do not slacken the pace for me unless I tell you.' (25) And she departed, and went to the man of God at Mount Carmel. So it was, when the man of God saw her afar off, that he said to his servant Gehazi, 'Look the Shunammite woman! (26) Please run now to meet her, and say to her, 'Is it well with you? Is it well with your husband? Is it well with the child?' And she answered, 'It is well.' (27) Now when she came to the man of God at the hill, she caught him by the feet, but Gehazi came near to push her away. But the man of God said, 'Let her alone; for her soul is in deep distress, and the Lord has hidden it from me, and has not told me.'" 2 Kings 4:18–27

Why did she become deeply distressed after being blessed with a child? (1)

According to Elisha what about her is in deep distress? _____(2)

Why do you think that God did not reveal her distress to Elisha? (3)

"When you are in distress, and all these things come upon you in the latter days, when you turn to the Lord your God and obey His voice, He will not forsake you nor destroy you, nor forget the covenant of your fathers which He swore to them." Deut.4:30

The Shunammite woman went directly to whom?_____(4)

Did she tell her husband?_____(5) **or Gehazi?**_____(5)

Why do you think that she did not tell her husband or Gehazi and went directly to Elisha?

Who do you run to when you are in deep distress?

Above in Deut.4:30 states who we should turn to in deep distress? (6)

"So she said, Did I ask a son of my lord? Did I not say, "Do not deceive me?"" 2 Kings 4:28

What do these words say about the death of her son? _____(7)

Who does she blame for the death?_____ (8)

Who does she go to for help?_____ (9)

What similarity do we do when something happens to us?

How are we similar in action to the Shunammite woman when tragedy happens?

Who do we blame and who do we go to?

"I called on the Lord in distress; the Lord answered me and set me in a broad place. The Lord is on my side; I will not fear. What can man do to me?" Ps. 118:5

Even when surrounded by impossible circumstances, we can proclaim that the Lord is on our side? **Distress** does not separate us from the love of Christ.

Paul says: "Who shall separate us from the love of Christ? Shall tribulation, or distress or persecution, or famine, or nakedness, or peril, or sword? For I am persuaded that neither death nor life, nor angels nor principalities nor powers, nor things present nor things to come, nor height nor depth, nor any other created thing, shall be able to separate us from the love of God which is in Christ Jesus our Lord." Romans 8:35-39

The Shunammite woman's ninth characteristic was her persistence.

She was PERSISTENT.

Read through 2 Kings 4:8-31 and match below areas where she was persistent:

Husband	persuaded him to eat
Elisha	to go and see Elisha
Gehazi	drive/forward/do not slack
Her Servant	to make an upper room
Elisha	to see Elisha
Husband	used familiar words

The Shunammite woman used familiar words to Elisha to reveal to him her spiritual need for his presence. These words were words he used to Elijah when Elisha would not leave Elijah's side.

Compare 2 Kings 4:30 to 2 Kings 2:2. What are the familiar words that she uses to Elisha:(10)

If you read forward in 2 Kings 2:6 and 2 Kings 2:10 Elisha repeats these words to Elijah three times.

"to self control, perseverance, to perseverance, godliness." 2 Peter 2:4

Where do you see the Shunammite woman having self control?

How did her self-control lead to perseverance?

The Shunammite woman exercised self-control. She did not easily succumb to discouragement or the temptation to quit. She viewed her circumstance as coming from the hand of a loving Father who is in control of all things.

This view is the secret of perseverance – to see all circumstances coming from the loving hand of God. The Parable of the persistent friend is found in Luke.

"And Jesus said to them, 'Which of you shall have a friend, and go to him at midnight and say to him, 'Friend, lend me three loaves, for a friend of mine has nothing to set before him; and he will answer from within and say, 'Do not trouble me. The door is now shut, and my children are with me in bed. I cannot rise and give to you?' I say to you, though he will not rise and give to him because he is his friend, yet because of his persistence he will rise and give him as many as he needs.' So I say to you, 'ask, and it will be given to you; seek, and you will find; knock, and it will be opened to you. For everyone who asks receives, and he who seeks finds, and to him who knocks it will be opened.'" Luke 11:5-10

Persistence in this friend, as in the Shunammite woman, is a shameless boldness. It is not tenacity. In this parable, Jesus' point is that in prayer, the disciple is to be bold. This man goes boldly to his neighbor to seek what he requires. Likewise, the Shunammite woman goes boldly to Elisha, Gehazi, her servant and her husband.(6)

Do you go boldly to God for that which is needed?

Who are you when you have needs? Do you ask, seek, and knock?

Begin to practice in prayer to boldly go to God asking Him to supply your needs. Seek what He has for you and receive God's spirit with what is spiritually beneficial.

"And not only that, but we also glory in tribulations, knowing that tribulation produces perseverance, and perseverance, character and character, hope." Romans 5:3

This scripture uses the word tribulation. Tribulation in this text means deep distress. Listen to the words now as I substitute deep distress where tribulation is recorded.

"And not only that, but we also glory in deep distress, knowing that deep distress produces perseverance, and perseverance, character and character, hope."

In these words do you see anything about the Shunammite woman?

She was in deep distress; it gave her persistence.

Who are you when in deep distress? Do you persevere? Write a prayer to ask, seek and knock to the Lord the areas of your life that are in deep distress.

"Praying always with all prayer and supplication in the Spirit, being watchful to this end with all perseverance and supplication for all the Saints." Eph.6:18

At the end of the story of the Shunammite woman, God gives her a son and heals her son through Elisha, we see God as a compassionate and merciful God.

"Indeed we count them blessed who endure. You have heard of the perseverance of Job and seen the end intended by the Lord– that the Lord is very compassionate and merciful." James 5:11

From the scripture above substitute the Shunammite woman for Job.

ANSWERS:

1. **Her son died**
2. **Her soul**
3. **Your opinion(to show God's Glory)**
4.. **Elisha, the man of God**
5. **No**
6. **Turn to the Lord God**
7. **Her pain in the death of her child was worse than the emptiness she felt before he was born**
8. **Elisha**
9. **Elisha**
10. **"As the Lord lives, and as your soul lives I will not leave you."**

THIS IS WHO WE ARE

We have been called to be different
We are disciples of Jesus Christ.

We carry all the family values..................in our hearts.
We carry the Holy Spirit..........................in our hearts.
We carry Jesus.......................................in our hearts.
We belong to Jesus................you cannot get out of it.
We carry where we come from................in our hearts.

Elisha

WEEK 2 DAY 1

This week we will continue our study looking at Elisha's relationship to the Shunammite woman.

There are 2 prophets with similar names, Elisha and Elijay. Both are prophets from God. So similar in name, that it can be confusing.

Here are some ways to help you remember the difference:

1) Elijah was first.
      His only letter difference is   (J), which comes before
      Elisha's letter difference with a   (S)
      (J) comes before   (S) alphabetically.

2) Elisha was Elijah's successor. 1 Kings 19:16–21
      Elisha is second to Elijah.
      The   (s) again could stand for second or successor.

3) Elisha is seen here with the Shunammite woman.
      Again a letter being similar.   (S)

4) Elijah appears with Jesus in the transfiguration.
      Letter similar   (J) Matt. 17:1–4

5) Elijah was taken_____(1) 2 Kings 2:1–15

6) Elisha_____(2)and has a miracle preformed from his bones. 2 Kings 13:14–21

Can you add more to the list:

In 2 Kings, Elisha asked the sons of the prophets to keep silent three times. I find it humorous that his name ends in 'sha', which is often used to silent others.

This scripture, **2 Kings 4:18-37** is our study base. Read the scripture and pay close attention to Elisha.

2 Kings 4: 8-37

"Now it happened one day that **Elisha** went to Shunem, where there was a notable woman, and she persuaded **him** to eat some food. So it was, as often as he passed by, **he** would turn in there to eat some food. And she said to her husband, 'Look now, I know that this is a **holy man of God**, who passes by us regularly. Please let us make a small upper room on the wall; and let us put a bed for **him** there, and a table and a chair and a lampstand; so it will be, whenever **he** comes to us, **he** can turn in there."

And it happened one day that **he** came there, and **he** turned into the upper room and lay down there. Then **he** said to Gehazi his servant, 'Call this Shunammite woman.' When he had called her, she stood before him. And he said to him, 'Say now to her,

'Look, you have been concerned for us with all this care. What can I do for you? Do you want me to speak on your behalf to the king or to the commander of the army?'"

She answered, 'I dwell among my own people.'

So **he** said, 'What then is to be done for her?'

And Gehazi answered, 'Actually she has no son, and her husband is old.'

So **he** said, 'Call her.' When he had called her, she stood in the doorway. Then **he** said,'About this time next year you shall embrace a son.'

And she said,'No, **my lord, man of God**, do not lie to your maid servant!'

But the woman conceived, and bore a son when the appointed time had come, of which **Elisha** had told her.

And the child grew. Now it happened one day that he went out to his father, to the reapers. And he said to his father, 'My head, my head!'

So he said to a servant, 'Carry him to his mother.' When he had taken him and brought him to his mother, he sat on her knees till noon, and then died. And she went up and laid him on the bed of the man of God, shut the door upon him, and went out. Then she called to her husband, and said,

'Please send me one of the young men and one of the donkeys, that I may run to the **man of God** and come back.'

So he said, 'Why are you going to him today? It is neither the New Moon nor the Sabbath."

And she said, 'It is well.' Then she saddled a donkey, and said to her servant, 'Drive, and go forward; do not slacken the pace for me unless I tell you.' And so she departed, and went to the **man of God** at Mount Carmel.

So it was, when the **man of God** saw her afar off, that **he** said to his servant Gehazi, 'Look, the Shunammite woman! Please run now to meet her, and say to her, 'Is it well with you? Is it well with your husband? Is it well with the child?'

And she answered, 'It is well.' Now when she came to the **man of God** at the hill, she caught **him** by the feet, but Gehazi came near to her to push her away. But the **man of God** said, 'Let her alone; for her soul is in deep distress, and the Lord has hidden it from me, and has not told me.'

So she said, 'Did I ask a son of **my lord**? Did I not say, 'Do not deceive me?'

Then **he** said to Gehazi, 'Get yourself ready, and take **my** staff in your hand, and be on your way. If you meet anyone, do not greet him; and if anyone greets you, do not answer him: but lay **my** staff on the face of the child.'

And the mother of the child said, **'As the Lord lives, and as your soul lives, I will not leave you.'** So **he** arose and followed her. Now Gehazi went on ahead of them, and laid the staff on the face of the child; but there was neither voice nor hearing. Therefore he went back to meet **him,** and told **him,** saying, 'The child has not awakened.'

When **Elisha** came into the house, there was the child, lying dead on his bed. **He** went in therefore, shut the door behind the two of them, and prayed to the Lord. And **he** went up and lay on the child, and put **his** mouth on his mouth, **his** eyes on his eyes, and **his** hands on his hands; and **he** stretched himself out on the child, and the flesh of the child became warm. **He** returned and walked back and forth in the house, and again went up and stretched **himself** out on him; then the child sneezed seven times and the child opened his eyes. And **he** called Gehazi and said, 'Call this Shunammite woman.'

So he called her. And when she came into **him**, **he** said, 'Pick up your son.' So she went in, fell at **his** feet, and bowed to the ground; then she picked up her son and went out."

Now- read : 1 Kings 17:8-24

"Then the word of the Lord came to him, saying, 'Arise, go to Zarephath, which belongs to Sidon, and dwell there. See, I have commanded a widow there to provide for you.' So he arose and went to Zarephath. And when he came to the gate of the city, indeed a widow was there gathering sticks. And he called to her and said, 'Please bring me a little water in a cup, that I may drink.' And as she was going to get it, he called to her and said, 'Please bring me a morsel of bread in your hand.'

So she said, '**As the Lord your God lives,** I do not have bread, only a handful of flour in a bin, and a little oil in a jar; and see, I am gathering a couple of sticks that I may go in and prepare it for myself and my son, that we may eat it, and die.'

And Elijah said to her, 'Do not fear; go and do as you have said, but make me a small cake from it first, and bring it to me; and afterward make some for yourself and your son. The bin of flour shall not be used up, nor shall the jar of oil run dry, until the day the Lord sends rain on the earth.'

So she went away and did according to the word of Elijah; and she and he and her household ate for many days. The bin of flour was not used up, nor did the jar of oil run dry, according to the word of the Lord which He spoke by Elijah.

Now it happened after these things that the son of the woman who owned the house became sick. And his sickness was so serious that there was not breath left in him. So she said to Elijah, 'What have I to do with you, O man of God? Have you come to me to bring my sin to remembrance, and to kill my son?'

And he said to her, 'Give me your son.' So he took him out of her arms and carried him to the upper room where he was staying, and laid him on his own bed. Then he cried out to the Lord and said, 'O Lord my God, have You also brought tragedy on the widow with whom I lodge by killing her son?" And he stretched himself out on the child three times and cried out to the Lord and said, "O Lord my God, I pray, let this child's soul come back to him.' Then the Lord heard the voice of Elijah; and the soul of the child came back to him, and he revived.

And Elijah took the child and brought him down from the upper room into the house, and gave him to his mother. And Elijah said, 'See your son lives.'

Then the woman said to Elijah, 'Now by this I know that you are a man of God, and that the word of the Lord in your mouth is the truth.'"

Compare the two relationships: Elisha and the woman at Shunem to Elijah and the widow of Zarephath,

Both the women at Shunem (2 Kings 4:30) and the widow at Zarephath (vs. 24) were taught the value of trusting in God alone.

Read these 2 verses(below) and see how both women asserted their faith in the living God:
~2 Kings 4:30, "And the mother of the child said 'As the Lord lives and as your soul lives, I will not leave you.'"
~1 Kings 17:24, "Then the woman said to Elijah, 'Now by this, I know that you are a man of God, and the word of the Lord in your mouth is truth.'"

When the widow says "Now...I know" her belief had grown into fullness of faith. Elijah had proved by word and deed. Both the widow and Elijah and the Shunammite woman's life and death and resurrection of their son's demonstrate that the Lord is the God of life itself.

Do you have that deep faith like these two women? Is this who you are?

Read 1 Kings 17:1
Elijah said to Ahab, "As the Lord God of Israel lives, before whom I stand, there shall not be dew nor rain these years, except at my word."

These words are a brilliant declaration from Elijah, who at the time stood unafraid before the king of Israel, unannounced and uninvited. He knew the glory, majesty and power of God were greater than Ahab's. The Shunammite women and the Zarephath widow knew also of God's glory, majesty and power.

Read 2 Kings 2:1-7

"And it came to pass, when the Lord was about to take up Elijah into heaven by a whirlwind the Elijah went with Elisha from Gilgal. Then Elijah said to Elisha, "Stay here, please, for the Lord has sent me down to Bethel.

Now the sons of the prophets who were at Bethel came out to Elisha, and said to him. 'Do you know that the Lord will take away your master from over you today?'

Then Elijah said to him, 'Elisha, stay here, please, for the Lord has sent me on to Jericho.'

But he said, 'As the Lord lives, and as your soul lives, I will not leave you!' So they came to Jericho.

Now the sons of the prophets who were at Jericho came to Elisha and said to him,' Do you know that the Lord will take away your master for over you today?'

So he answered, 'Yes, I know, keep silent!'

Then Elijah said to him, "Stay here please, for the Lord has sent me on to the Jordan."

But he said, 'As the Lord lives, and as your soul lives, I will not leave you.' And fifty men of the sons of the prophets went and stood facing them at a distance, while the two of them stood by the Jordan."

How does Elisha respond to Elijah when Elijah states that the Lord is sending him to Bethel, Jericho and Jordan?

2 Kings 2:2 – Elisha says to Elijah, 'As the Lord lives, and as your soul lives, I will not leave you!'
2 Kings 2:4 – Elisha says to Elijah, 'As the Lord lives, and as your soul lives, I will not leave you!'
2 Kings 2:6 – Elisha says to Elijah, 'As the Lord lives and as your soul lives, I will not leave you!'

How many times does Elisha state this to Elijah?_____(3)

Elisha made a solemn promise three times in these verses. He determined that he would remain by his master Elijah no matter what might occur.

Go back up to our main text, 2 Kings 4:8–12 and under line these same words.

Elisha hears his same words that he spoke to Elijah from the Shunammite woman. **What thoughts do you think Elisha had when he heard these same words?**

With this oath, the Shunammite woman asserted her faith in the living God. Let us assert our faith in the living God in prayer and the study of His word.

Prayer: Help us in this study to become more aware of the light of our Lord that is ever present in all we do, that we will allow our vessel to be open to Him. Allow His light to enter and fill you with His love and mercy.

ANSWERS:

1. Up to Heaven
2. Dies
3. Elijah states three times to Elisha, "As the Lord Lives, and as your soul lives, I will not leave you!"
4. 3

Elijah

WEEK 2 DAY 2

It is Elisha with the Shunammite woman.

It is Elijah with Moses who appears on the Mount of Transfiguration with Jesus (Matt 17:3).

Elijah important to us in this study because he mentors Elisha.

Elijah's prophetic ministry is seen with miracles of feeding people with small amounts of food and raising a child from the dead.

Of whom does his ministry remind you?_____(1)

To remember the difference between the two, we took the middle letter of their name to symbolize a comparison:

Elijah's J comes before Elisha's S. Elijah was first. Elisha was second.

Elijah appears with Jesus in the New Testament.

The J is another good reminder of Elijah with Jesus.

In 856 B.C., Elijah begins to prophesy against Ahab.

Ahab was a wicked king. God sends Elijah, a man more than equal to the task, to take on Ahab. Elijah is described as Israel's greatest and most dramatic prophet over the very lowest point in the degeneration of the spiritual life of the kings of Israel. (NKJV Study Bible pg 551)

If we did a running graph, we would dip the scale at its lowest and this time line depth would show where Israel was when God sends Elijah, the Prophet, to the king of Israel, Ahab.

King Ahab acted as though sin was trival. First, he married a foreign wife. Second, he made the national religion Baal. You may be familiar with his foreign wife. Her name is _____(2) . (see the scripture below)

Read 1 Kings 16:30-31

"Now Ahab the son Omri did evil in the sight of the Lord more than all who were before him. And it came to pass, as though it had been a trivial thing, for him to walk in the sins of Jeroboam the son of Nebat, that he took as wife Jezebel the daughter of Ethbaal, king of the Sidonians; and he went and served Baal and worshiped him."

Who are you in your marriage or your relationship closest to you?

Biblically, the leader is the man. Reality is that with or without a spiritual leader, women have a strong influence. Jezebel changed Ahab.

Ahab the king of Israel broke covenant with God.

First– King Ahab put another god before God; **This god was _____(3)**

King Ahab breaks the first commandment which is _____4)

Second– He married Jezebel, a foreigner.

Is your influence to things in your home positive?

Is your influence Spiritual?

Who are you in relationship to God?

Is He first or is He treated as a trivial thing?

Do you allow other gods to come before the one true God?

What can you do to influence your home to make God the center of all things:

Jezebel's influence over king Ahab turned Ahab's god to Baal. Ahab is king over Israel. Jezebel becomes the queen, a foreigner, who influenced Ahab to turn to other gods.

At Mount Carmel Elijah displayed the unforgettable power of God over the false god Baal and his four hundred fifty prophets. In 1 Kings 18:22 Elijah stood **alone** ready to confront **450** prophets of Baal.

"Then Elijah said to the people, 'I alone am left a prophet of the Lord; but Baal's prophets are 450 men'."

Read the rest of the story 1 Kings 18:22-40

Vs 23: "Therefore let them give us two bulls; and let them choose one bull for themselves, cut it in pieces, and lay it on the wood, but put no fire under it; and I will prepare the other bull, and lay it on the wood, but put no fire under it.

Then you call on the name of the gods; and I will call on the name of the Lord; and the God who answers by fire, He is God."

So all the people answered and said, 'it is well spoken.'

Now Elijah said to the prophets of Baal, 'Choose one bull for yourselves and prepare it first, for you are many; and call on the name of your god, but put no fire under it.'

So they took the bull which was given them, and they prepared it, and called on the name of Baal from morning even till noon, saying, 'O Baal, hear us!' But there was no voice; no one answered. Then they leaped about the altar which they had made.

And so it was, at noon, that Elijah mocked them and said, 'Cry aloud, for he is a god; either he is meditating, or he is busy, or he is on a journey, or perhaps he is sleeping and must be awakened.' So they cried aloud, and cut themselves, as was their custom, with knives and lances, until the blood gushed out on them. And when midday was past, they prophesied until the time of the offering of the evening sacrifice. But there was no voice; no one answered, no one paid attention.

Then Elijah said to all the people, 'Come near to me.' So all the people came near to him. And he repaired the altar of the Lord that was broken down. And Elijah took twelve stones, according to the number of the tribes of the sons of Jacob, to whom the word of the Lord had come, saying 'Israel shall be your name.' Then with the stones he built an altar in the name of the Lord; and he made a trench around the altar large enough to hold two seahs of seed. And he put the wood in order, cut the bull in pieces, and laid it on the wood, and said, 'Fill your water pots with water, and pour it on the burnt sacrifice and on the wood.' Then he said, 'Do it a second time,' and they did it a second time; and he said, 'Do it a third time', and they did it a third time. So the water ran all around the altar; and he also filled the trench with water.

And it came to pass, at the time of the offering of the evening sacrifice, that Elijah the prophet came near and said, 'Lord God of Abraham, Isaac, and Israel, let it be known this day that You are God in Israel and I am Your servant and that I have done all these things at Your word. Hear me, O Lord, hear me, that this people may know that You are the Lord God, and that You have turned their hearts back to You again.'

Then the fire of the Lord fell and consumed the burnt sacrifice, and the wood and the stones and the dust, and it licked up the water that was in the trench. Now when all the people saw it, they fell on their faces; and they said, 'The Lord, He is God! The Lord, He is God!'

And Elijah said to them, 'Seize the prophets of Baal! Do not let one of them escape!' So they seized them and Elijah brought them down to the Brook of Kishon and executed them there."

This story of God working through Elijah is powerful.

The fire consumes even the dust. This consumption shows that God's power is over everything, even the dust.

Elijah's prayer asked not just for the fire to consume but for God to reveal Himself to clearly show the people that God alone is the living God and to revive the people to see God as their God.

Prayer: God reveal in our life Your light to show others that we love the Lord God of Abraham, Isaac, and Israel. Please consume even the smallest of sin in our life. We declare in our hearts and to our families that "The Lord, He is God."

The story of Elijah continues tomorrow when we will see his inter action with Elisha. If you want to read more about Elijah continue to read 1 Kings 18:40–19:18.

ANSWERS:

1. Jesus
2. Jezebel
3. Baal
4. "Though shall not have any other god's before me" Exodus 20

Elijah Ascends To Heaven

WEEK 2 DAY 3

Our study of the Shunammite woman continues today looking at the relationship between Elijah and Elisha.

2 Kings 2:1-18

"And it came to pass, when the Lord was about to take up Elijah into heaven by a whirlwind, that Elijah went with Elisha from Gilgal. Then Elijah said to Elisha, 'Stay here, please, for the Lord has sent me on to Bethel.'

But Elisha said, 'As the Lord lives, and as your soul lives, I will not leave you!' So they went down to Bethel.

3)Now the sons of the prophets who were at Bethel came out to Elisha, and said to him, 'Do you know that the Lord will take away your master from over you today?'

And he said, 'Yes, I know; keep silent!'

Then Elijah said to him, 'Elisha, stay here, please, for the Lord has sent me on to Jericho.'

But he said, 'As the Lord lives, and so your soul lives, I will not leave you!' So they came to Jericho.

5)Now the sons of the prophets who were at Jericho came to Elisha and said to him. 'Do you know that the Lord will take away your master from over you today?'

So he answered, 'Yes, I know: keep silent!'

Then Elijah said to him, 'Stay here, please, for the Lord has sent me on to the Jordan.'

But he said, 'As the Lord lives and as your soul lives, I will not leave you!' So the two of them went on. (7)And fifty men of the sons of the prophets went and stood facing them at a distance, while the two of them stood by the Jordan. Now Elijah took his mantle, rolled it up, struck the water; and it was divided this way and that, so that the two of them crossed over on dry ground.

And so it was, when they had crossed over, that Elijah said to Elisha, 'Ask! What may I do for you, before I am taken away from you?'

Elisha said, 'Please let a double portion of your spirit be upon me.'

So he said, 'You have asked a hard thing. Nevertheless, if you see me when I am taken from you, it shall be so for you; but if not, it shall not be so.' Then it happened, as they continued on and talked, that suddenly a chariot of fire appeared with horses of fire, and separated the two of them; and Elijah went up by a whirlwind into heaven.

And Elisha saw it, and he cried out, 'My father, my father, the chariot of Israel and its horse men!' So he saw him no more. And he took hold of his own clothes and tore them into two pieces. He also took up the mantle of Elijah that had fallen from him, and went back and stood by the bank of the Jordan."

Then he took the mantle of Elijah that had fallen from him, and struck the water, and said, "Where is the Lord God of Elijah?" And when he also had struck the water, it was divided this way and that; and Elisha crossed over.

Now when the sons of the prophets who were from Jericho saw him, they said, 'The spirit of Elijah rest on Elisha.' And they came to meet him, and bowed to the ground before him'.

Name the cities where Elijah and Elisha were going – from there beginning:

Gilgal, (1)   (2)   (3)

What were the words that Elijah repeated to Elisha on each travel call? (4)

What was Elisha's response each time?(5)

What do Elisha's words say about how he felt toward Elijah?

Elisha made a solemn promise to Elijah. Elisha was determined that he would remain by his master no matter what occurred.

Elijah and Elisha cross over the divided water and Elijah says:

"Ask! What may I do for you, before I am taken away from you?"

Does Elijah say before I die?_____(6)

From all you have read, do you think that all involved knew that Elijah would be taken? Even Elijah?

Look at 2 Kings 2:3

What are the words that the sons of the prophets say who were in Bethel say to Elisha ?(7)

Look at 2 Kings 2:5

What are the words that the sons of the prophets say who were in Jericho say to Elisha?(8)

The sons of the prophets who stood before them by the **Jordan** are not specific to what prophets but the scripture does say how many?_____(9) 2 Kings 2:7

The last passage does tell us where the prophets were from?(10)

It is the sons of the prophets who were in_____ (11)

Who saw Elisha and declare:(12)

The sons of the prophets came to Elisha each time when they entered the city of Bethel and Jericho. What were their words to Elisha?_____(13)

What was Elisha's answer to them?_____(14)

Why do you think Elisha wanted these men to keep silent?

2 Kings 2:9 "and so it was, when they had crossed over, that Elijah said to Elisha,"Ask! What may I do for you, before I am taken away from you?"

Elisha said, "Please let a double portion of your spirit be upon me."

What does Elisha ask for from Elijah?_____(15)

Was his request for things or for his spirit?_____(16)

Twice as many miracles are narratively reported for Elisha than Elijah but Elisha's request was that he would be Elijah's spiritual successor. Double portion was a mark of the father's blessing among sons. This portion was an ancient Middle Eastern custom that the first born would receive double portions.

In Deut. 21:17 Jacob gives Joseph the double portion. Reuben, the firstborn of Jacob, forfeited because of his disreputable behavior.

Elisha wanted a double portion of Elijah's spirit. His request is **not** due to pride. He simply wanted to be the man of God who would follow Elijah's spirit.

How many were in the last group of the sons of the prophets?_____(17)

What did they do?_____(18)

Look at 2 Kings 2:16–18"

Then they said to him, "Look now, there are fifty strong men with your servants. Please let them go and search for your master, lest perhaps the Spirit of the Lord has taken him up and cast him upon some mountain or into some valley."

And he said, "You shall not send anyone."

But when they urged him till he was ashamed, he said, "Send them!" Therefore they sent fifty men, and they searched for three days but did **not** find him. And when they came back to him, for he had stayed in Jericho, he said to them, **"Did I not say to you, 'Do not go?'"**

How many men were sent to look for Elijah against Elisha's judgement?
_____(19)

2 Kings 2:17 "But when they urged him till he was ashamed he said, "Send them!" Therefore they sent fifty men, and they searched for three days but did not find him"

Groups of 50 strong men were often called upon to perform an arduous task.

Were the search team of 50 and the 50 sons of the prophets the same men?_____ (20)

The 50 who watched were 50 "sons of the prophets". The other 50 men, "strong men" were with Elisha's servants. He traveled with a posse.

Look at 2 Kings 2:7 "And fifty of the sons of the prophets went and stood facing them at a distance, while the two of them stood by the Jordan."

These men knew what would happen because God had sent them a revelation that Elijah would be taken to heaven. Still they sent 50 men to search for Elijah. They wanted proof of his departure.

How many days did they search?_____ (21)   (2 Kings 2:17)

Three days is referenced many times in the Bible as a significant time. Jesus spoke in Matthew 12:40 "For as Jonah was three days and three nights in the belly of the great fish, so will the Son of Man be three days and three nights in the heart of the earth."

In ancient Israel, a part of a day was considered a whole day. So a period of 26 hours could be called three days.

Do you think that that 50 men and the three day search is significant?

What would your response be if you were Elisha and the master you had begun to follow(that you left your parents and work for) is going to leave you?

Have you been or are you going through this now where someone you dearly love is going to leave or has left?

God prepares our hearts. He gives us the knowledge to deal with circumstances through His will and His comfort. It might not be before it happens or when it happens but He is shaping and molding you to become the person He wants you to be. If your heart is heavy, lean on Him.

2 Kings 2:13-14 "He also took up the mantle of Elijah that had fallen from him, and went back and stood by the bank of the Jordan. Then he took the mantle of

Elijah that had fallen from him, and struck the water, and said, 'Where is the Lord God of Elijah?' And when he also had struck the water, it was divided this way and that; and Elisha crossed over."

The word mantle kept me tossing and turning one night. Mantle to me is what is over the fireplace. Seems rather large for Elijah to carry with him. And Elijah roles it up.

Further investigation and lots of prayer revealed that the mantle was only a symbol, but in the hands of Elijah it had been an instrument for the power of the living God. The mantle had been for Elijah what the rod had been for Moses and Aaron.

The mantle as the rod of Moses and Aaron was the symbol of God's power in the hands of who held it. The rod was to demonstrate the reality of His power and presence during Moses' coming mission. Aaron's rod would figure prominently in several of the plaques. This rod was the same that was lifted while Moses stretched out his hand for the sea to divide for the children of Israel to go over dry ground through the midst of the sea.(NKJV Study Bible pg 568)

Recall Exodus 4:1-5

"Then Moses answered and said, "But suppose they will not believe me or listen to my voice; suppose they say, 'The Lord has not appeared to you.'"

So the Lord said to him, "What is that in your hand?"

He said,"A rod."

And He said, "Cast it on the ground". So he cast it on the ground, and it became a serpent; and Moses fled from it. Then the Lord said to Moses, "Reach out your hand and take it by the tail"(and he reached out his hand and caught it, and it became a rod in his hand,) "that they may believe that the Lord God of Isaac, and the God of Jacob, has appeared to you."

Exodus 7:9 "When Pharaoh speaks to you, saying, 'Show a miracle for yourselves', then you shall say to Aaron, 'Take your rod and cast it before Pharaoh, and let it become a serpent.'"

Exodus 14:16 "But lift up your rod, and **stretch out your hand over the sea and divide it. ....**"

In 1 Kings 19:19 Elijah had laid the mantle on Elisha as a symbolic action.

Now in 2 Kings 2:13 Elisha took up the prophetic status and ministry that the mantle symbolized.

1 Kings 19:19 "So he departed from there, and found Elisha the son of Shaphat, who was plowing with twelve yoke of oxen before him, and he was with the twelfth. Then Elijah passed by him and threw his mantle on Elisha."

2 Kings 2:13-14 "He also took up the mantle of Elijah that had fallen from him, and went back and stood by the bank of the Jordan. Then he took the mantle of Elijah that had fallen from him, and struck the water, and said, 'Where is the Lord God of Elijah?' And when he also **had struck the water, it was divided this way and that; and Elisha crossed over.'**

Compare these two verses Exodus 14:16 (above) and 2 Kings 2:14(above)

Elisha struck the water with the mantle and the water divided. Do you believe this was a conformation from God that Elisha is the new successor following Elijah?

The water was the Jordan River, somewhere near Jericho. Elijah was like Moses in that his life and ministry show many parallels to that of Israel's greatest prophet. As Moses had divided the waters of the Red Sea in the final act of the redemption of Israel from Egypt, so now Elijah replicated this miracle by dividing the waters of the Jordan. The difference is that Elijah did not use the power of God as a great redeeming miracle as Moses had done, but as an almost casual demonstration of God's wonders as he was walking on his way. Elisha takes up this same symbol of God's power.

We are the sons of God. We possess His power.

Prayer: Help us to be aware of God's power that lives within us. We ask that God's power be revealed to us. Increase our knowledge that our mighty God loves and adores us. We are the sons and daughters of Him. We do possess His power. Amen

ANSWERS:

1. **Bethel**
2. Jericho
3. Jordan
4. Stay here, please for the Lord has sent me to.....vs:2; vs:4; vs:6
5. As the Lord lives and as your soul lives, I will not leave you.vs:2; vs:4
6. NO. "Before I am taken"
7. Take Away--Do you know that the Lord will take away your master.
8. Take away "Do you know that the Lord will take away your master from over you today?
9. 50
10. Jericho
11. "The spirit of Elijah rests on Elisha."
12. "Do you know that the Lord will take away your master from over you today?"
13. "Do you know that the Lord will take away your master from over you today?"
14. "Yes, I know keep silent"
15. "Please let a double portion of your spirit be upon me"
16. the spirit
17. 50
18. Sons of the prophets of Jordan~ They went and stood facing them at a distance, while the two of them stood by the Jordan. So they witnessed the actual event.
19. 50
20. No
21. 3

Elisha Begins His Miracles

WEEK 2 DAY 4

The Shunammite woman is introduced this week in our study to Elisha. He has taken the place of Elijah who was taken up by the Lord.

Elisha asked to be blessed with a double portion from Elijay. Recorded in the bible Elisha's miracles outnumber Elijah's. Here are some:

~Elisha parted the Jordan as Elijah had done previously.
~Elisha purified the water in Jericho.
~Elisha heard some young people call out to him in disbelief of Elijah's going up to heaven and he put a curse on them when they uttered the words, "Go up, you baldhead" causing 2 female bears to maul the 42 youths.
~Elisha achieved an atmosphere free of war for Jehoshaphat so Jehoshaphat, the king could concentrate on the divine revelation being revealed to him.
~Elisha provided water for Jehosphaphat's army when there was none to be found.
~Elisha gave prophetic instructions that the Lord will deliver the Moabites to Jehoshaphat.
~Elisha provided oil for the widow with two sons.
~Elisha raised the Shunammite's woman son.
~Elisha purified the Pot of Stew.
~Elisha fed one hundred men with a small amount of food.
~Elisha healed Naaman, commander of the army of the king of Syria, of leprosy.

Elisha did many things like calling for a musician in an effort to achieve an atmosphere free of strife so that the king might concentrate on the anticipated divine revelation. Elisha gave light to people in his time.

You will notice that many of the miracles carry instructions for the human involved.

Naaman was prideful but his men convinced him to follow Elishas' instructions. Man's faith and obedience are part of divine provision.

Elisha's miracles begin in 2 Kings 2 through 2 Kings 8. The scripture is full of Elisha's prophetic work which gives an understanding of who Elisha is in the story which emphasizes his importance of his prophetic office in ancient Israel.

The story told in 2 Kings 8 is a reappearance of the Shunammite woman.

Read below 2 Kings 8:1-6. Pay attention to the instructions given to her. In obediance she is faithful and a miracle is given:

"Then Elisha spoke to the woman whose son he had restored to life, saying, '**Arise** and **go,** you and your household, and **stay** wherever you can; for the Lord has called for a famine, and furthermore, it will come upon the land for seven years.'" So the woman arose and did according to the saying of the man of God, and she went with her household and dwelt in the land of the Philistines seven years.

It came to pass, at the end of **seven** years, that the woman returned from the land of the Philistines; and she went to make an appeal to the king for her house and for her land. Then the king talked with Gehazi, the servant of the man of God, saying, "Tell me, please, all the great things Elisha has done: Now it happened, as he was telling the king how he had restored the dead to life, that there was the woman whose son he had restored to life, appealing to the king for her house and for her land. And Gehazi said, "My lord, O king, this is the woman, and this is her son whom Elisha restored to life." And when the king asked the woman, she told him.

So the king appointed a certain officer for her, saying, "Restore all that was hers, and all the proceeds of the field from that day that she left the land until now."

What would you do if the Lord instructed you to suddenly move your entire household to another land?

Look at Matthew 3:13-15

"...an angel of the Lord appeared to Joseph in a dream, saying, "**Arise, take** the young child and His mother, **flee** to Egypt and **stay** there until I bring you word:"

Compare this scripture to the words Elisha uses in 2 Kings 8:1-6 above. Look at the following words and note the similarities.

Arise
Take
Go or Flee
Stay

Matthew's scripture is the 2nd of eleven prophecies fulfilled about Jesus' birth. This particular one comes out of Hosea 11:1 which says the Messiah would also come from Egypt.

We see the prophet, Elisha, instructing the Shunnamite woman to arise, take, go and stay in 2 Kings because of the prophesy he received about the famine. Joseph arises, takes Jesus and Mary, goes to Egypt and stays to flee from Herod until Herod dies.

Joseph and the Shunammite women were obedient to God's instructions.

The Shunammite woman returned in_____years(7). She had not renounced or sold her property but merely left during the previous famine.

Who did she press her claim to for the property?_____(2)

Seven years to claim her property is within the required time as seen in Deut 15:1-6; Ruth 4:3 and 4

Gehazi is telling the story when who arrives?_____(3)

Do you think that Gehazi is still loyal to Elisha?
Write the story that Gehazi tells:

In our study of her characteristics we saw that the woman was notable. Here in the story above, what words would you describe the woman of Shunammite as being?

4) additional in answers

There is no mention of her husband. Remember he was old. What do you think happened to him?

We assume she is a widow. Elisha asked her to take "you and your household" and "stay wherever you can." First you have to go. Go now. You will be gone for seven years in a foreign land.

Do you remember that she was a dweller? Now, she will dwell in Philistine. **Has God ever sent you, now, with your family to dwell in an area you are not accustomed to dwell?**

God asked us to arise and go, to tell others of who He is for He is the Light of the world. We are to bear witness of His Light. "In Him was life, and the life was the light of men. And the light shines in the darkness, and the darkness did not comprehend it........bear witness of this Light." John 1:4-8

We see the 7 years of famine pass before the Shunammite woman. God was good to her. Whether long term or short term, God is good to us.

5)**The climatic moment in her life was:**

What has been your climatic moment that God restored you and gave you hope for the future and showed you that God is good in all things and all the time?

God has brought me through seven years of many hard times. God has given me love abundantly. He never left me. He allowed His light to shine in me and He became my King.

David asked this Question in 2 Sam 7:18-19 He ask "Who am I?"

God answered by giving David the Davidic covenant that binds the heart of man to God.

The promise of a leader.
The promise of a king forever.
The King of the Jews who is?_____(6)
Is there a king of Israel now?_____(7)

Jesus is the King of All Kings.
No more kings.

Jesus is King eternal.
He is the Light of the World.

Understand your place. God may bring you from a mighty long way but this is who you are. God is with you now and He will bring you further.

Ebenezer means 'this far."

God has been with us "...this far." One day at a time. I can imagine that the Shunammite woman, a widow at the time, continued daily to say, one day at a time. She knew that it would be seven years because Elisha had told her. She knew the light of God was in her.

Pray today that God's light will shine brightly in you to reveal to others His love.

ANSWERS:

1. **Seven**
2. **The king**
3. **The Shunammite woman**
4. **Obedient when Elisha asked her to leave;**
   Bold to ask the king for what was hers;
   Dweller– again– in Philistine
   Loyal– to her country
5. **When the power of God thru Elisha restores her son**
6. **Jesus**
7. **No**

Elijah, Elisha and The Shunammite Woman

WEEK 2 DAY 5

Today is our last day that we study about how these two prophets connect to the Shunammite woman. In our study this week, we have seen some significant characteristics of Elijah and Elisha.

We know the difference between the two prophets Elijah and Elisha. We saw how Elisha received the blessings of double the portions to Elijah. We learned how the Shunammite woman was obedient to Elisha during the famine and because of her obedience she received a double portion of blessings after the famine.

Looking back on your life, do you see any seven year period of time where you went through famine and then at the end of the seven, God gave you blessings exceedingly?

Were there significant people that God put in your life that made you deal with your circumstances and others who guided you along the path?

Do you believe this time made you 'who you are' and put more of God's light within you so that you could share His goodness to others? Or do you believe that you were crushed and destroyed inside and God did not help you through this time of famine?

Share your experience:

Rev. 11:4-6 "These are the two olive trees and the two lampstands standing before the God of the earth. And if anyone wants to harm them, fire proceeds from their mouth and devours their enemies. And if anyone wants to harm them, he must be killed in this manner. These have power to shut heaven, so that no rain falls in the days of their prophecy; and they have power over waters to turn them to blood and to strike the earth with all plagues as often as they desire."

Re-read the words above and think about Elijah and Moses as you read.

In Rev. 11:4-6 the two unnamed witnesses are strikingly similar to Elijah and Moses. These two appeared together with Christ on the Mount of Transfiguration. They are named in Revelation as the two olive trees and two lamp stands linking them to the vision in Zech. 4:14 of "the two anointed ones, who stand beside the Lord of the whole earth".

In Zech. the two anointed ones are Zerubbabel and Joshua the priest. Over all is the witnesses for the Lord, who give their testimony to the truth.

The truth in Zech 4:6 says powerful words that their testimony to the truth is

"Not by power, but by MY SPIRIT."

When we are in God's Spirit, the Holy Spirit, He leads, guides and directs us. Not just through daily happenings but also through large overwhelming life experiences. This scripture points out to us that the rebuilding of the temple would be accomplished not by human strength or resources, but by the power of God's Spirit.

It is simple. When we allow God's Strength and His Resources to accomplish what His will for us will be, then overwhelming life experiences become easy.

The Shunammite woman put her trust in Elisha, the man of God, because she had great faith that he could transform her life from the devastation that was before her.

First~She does not expect a child~a son.
Second~She places the fate of her son on Elisha
Third~She loses all her possessions

FIRST: She did not expect a son and had thrown the thought to the wayside;
  She was_____ (1)

2 Kings 4:14"..She has no son, and her husband is old."

She responded:
2 Kings 4:16 "No, my lord. Man of God, do not lie to your maidservant!"
Why do you think she had doubt:

Do you doubt the impossible? The Shunammite woman felt that even Elisha
could not fulfill such a promise. Compare the announcement to the story of Isaac to Abraham and Sarah in Gen. 21.
Do you remember what Sarah did when God promised her a son?(2)

Why was it so hard for Sarah to believe she would conceive?(3)

Why was it so hard for the Shunammite woman do believe that she would conceive?(4)
Can you see how their circumstances would cause them to doubt what God was about to do?

By means of God's mercy, she had gained her son.
Nothing is impossible with God.

From The Message:
"Seek My Face, and you will find all that you have longed for.
The deepest yearnings of your heart are for intimacy with Me.
I know, because I designed you to desire Me. Do not feel guilty about taking time
to be still in My Presence. You are simply responding to the tugs of divinity within
you. I made you in My image, and I hid heaven in your heart.
Your yearning for Me is a form of homesickness: longing for your true home
in heaven."

SECOND: She places the fate of her son on Elisha.
What happened to her son?_____(5)2 Kings 4:19-20
Where did she place the child's body?_____(6)2 Kings 4:21
Despite her overwhelming sorrow she places the fate of her child to Elisha.
The impossible is accomplished.

Elijah's story of reviving the widow's son in 1 Kings 17:17–24 and Elisha's story of reviving the son of the Shunammite woman are very similar.

Both women's belief had grown into a fullness of faith.

God is the author of life itself.

THIRD: The Shunammite woman loses all her possessions.

What was the nature of her leaving Shunem?_____(7)

2 Kings 8:1–6

Who did she take?_____(8)

How long did she stay?_____(9)

God in His kindness spared and restored the family of the Shunammite woman.

Think of this: She was barren, she had a son;

Her son died for no reason, raised to life again;

She lost all her earthly possessions, all restored plus more.

Do any of these words have a familiar ring:

Jesus came to bring light to all of us. He speaks in Luke 2:32 and says:

"A light to bring revelation to the Gentiles, And the glory of Your people Israel."

This scripture is the first to bring a statement that includes both Jew and Gentile salvation. Salvation is portrayed as a light. Luke 1:79

"To give light to those who sit in darkness and the shadow of death.
To guide our feet into the way of peace."

Elijah is compared to John the Baptist to be the messenger and prepare the way before Jesus. Elisha is compared to the Christ to bring light in the darkness to all.

Prayer:Christ,our Messiah, Jesus our Lord will provide the light of truth and forgiveness to those blinded by the darkness of their sins. Allow Him to shine His light through you that you will rest in Him and shine to others.

Answers:

1. Childless

2. She laughed – she did not believe
3. Her age
4. Her husbands age
5. Died with a headache
6. Laid him on the bed of man of God
7. Elisha tells her for there will be a famine in the land of Shunem
8. Her household
9. 7 years

God's Plan For You

I pray for you as you study. Pray today that God's light will shine brightly in you to reveal to others His love.

**Who are you? Are you a doer of the word? If God ask you to
ARISE, TAKE, GO, STAY-- are you willing?
Are you willing to be obedient to Him.**

Let God's plan for you be His plan; not your plan for God.

Relinquish control. God is trustworthy and He will provide. God blesses us with blessings. God's biggest blessing is Christ.

Realize God only does good things for us.

God's will is good. Romans 12:2 "Do not be conformed to this world, but be transformed by the renewing of your mind, that you may prove what is that good and acceptable and perfect will of God."

God's purpose is good. Phil 2:13 "For it is God who works in you both to will and to do for his good pleasure."

God's work for us is good. Phil 1:6 "Being confident of this very thing, that He who has begun a good work in you will complete it until the day of Jesus Christ."

God's hope for us is good. 2 Thes. 2:16 "Now may our Lord Jesus Christ Himself, and our God and Father, who has loved us and given us everlasting consolation and good hope by grace, comfort your hearts and establish you in every good word and work."

God's works that He created was good. Eph 2:10 "For we are His workmanship, created in Christ Jesus for good works, which God prepared beforehand that we should walk in them."

God's fight 1 Tim 1:18-19 "This charge I commit you according to the prophecies previously made concerning you, that by them you may wage the good warfare, having faith and a good conscience......"

God's fruits James 3:17 "But the wisdom that is from above is first pure, then peaceable, gentle, willing to yield, full of mercy and good fruits, without partiality and without hypocrisy."

God's everything Heb 13:16 "But do not forget to do good and to share, for with such sacrifices God is well pleased."

All things are good Romans 8:28 "And we know that all things work together for good to those who love God, to those who are the called according to His purpose."

The Bible is the good news. Read it. Study it. Mediate in it. For God speaks to us and shows His Light to us through His word.

"We who love the Lord, take the Bible straight, love one another and spread the gospel– you there, we here – we are all part of a great story of divine redemption sweeping through this sinful and exhausted world since the first coming of Christ." Ray and Jani Ortlund.

2 Samuel 22:29 "For You are my lamp, O Lord; The Lord shall enlighten my darkness."

From my favorite spiritual writer in Disciplines of A Beautiful Woman:

> The light of God surrounds me;
> The love of God enfolds me;
> The power of God protects me;
> The presence of God watches over me;
> Where ever I am, God is.
>
> Anne Ortlund

The Upper Room

WEEK 3 DAY 1

This is Who We Are; How We Become The Sons of God is the title of the book that my friend and my sons mother-in-love wrote. Her name is Roma Beth Bonner.

Our study is based on her book. From page 52, Beth writes:

"The Shunammite woman we read about truly displays for us a wealth of crucial information about how to sacrifice in order to apprehend and continue all we will ever need.

> "I am certain," said the woman to her husband, "I know that this man is a holy man of God, who passes by us regularly. Please, let us make a small upper room on the wall: and let us put a bed for him there, and a table and a chair and a lampstand; so it will be, whenever he comes to us, he can turn in there." 2 Kings 4:9-10

She knew if she built it, he would come.

No matter how passionate we may or may not be about apprehending God's provisions and blessings in our lives, the same is true across the board, we must make room for them. It is the belief in this truth, that if we open ourselves and start making a new place, new things will come, new things will begin to manifest, new things which ultimately take us to our destiny." Beth Bonner – **This is Who We Are; Becoming the Sons of God**

Our study for this week begins with the upper room and the Shunammite woman's preparation for Elisha.

The Shunammite woman was concerned with the normal measures of hospitality.

The quarters she requested from her husband was an upper room commonly on the roof and could be reached from the outside. This accommodated the guest while providing privacy. Look at the scriptures for the reality of this story:

2 Kings 4:8 "Now it happened one day that Elisha went to Shunem, where there was a notable woman, and she persuaded him to eat some food."

2 Kings 4:11 "And it happened one day that he came there, and he turned in to the upper room and lay down there."

2 Kings 4:18 "And the child grew. Now it happened one day that he went out to his father, to the reapers."

Look at the prefix in these scriptures:

2 Kings 4:8_____ **(1)**
2 Kings 4:11_____**(2)**
2 Kings 4:18_____**(3)**

Each prefix goes further to say "Now it happened"(4)

In the Gospels "Now it happened" is used to voice the truth of an actual event. Parables were told with a prefix of "the parable of." But here in the Old Testament it is told not as a parable but an actual event. "Now it Happened"...... Words of truth.

Elisha enters the city of Shunem where this notable women of Shunem has received permission from her husband and added an upper room for Elisha. In ancient cities the coolest place in the house was on the roof.

Judges 3:23 refers to it as the "cool chambers".

In 2 Kings 1:2, Ahaziah fell through the lattice of his upper room. It was common for the upper stories to have balconies enclosed with latticework, allowing for the flow of air while maintaing protection from the sun and a certain privacy.

In Daniel 6:10; Daniel knelt and prayed in his upper room toward Jerusalem. Three times a day he knelt and prayed at the windows facing Jerusalem.

Mark 14:13-16: The upper room we are all familiar with is where Christ is with his disciples for the passover celebration. In this scripture Jesus has sent two disciples to the city where a man will meet them and he will be carrying a pitcher of water. These disciples should follow him and the two disciples will speak to the master of the home.

vs 13) "And He sent out two of his disciples and said to them, "Go into the city, and a man will meet you carrying a pitcher of water; follow him. 14)Wherever he goes in, say to the master of the house, 'The Teacher says, "Where is the guest room in which I may eat the Passover with My disciples?" 15)Then he will show you a large upper room, furnished and prepared; there make ready for us.16) So His disciples went out, and came into the city and found it just as He had said to them; and they prepared the Passover."

The question they asked the master of the house was:(5)

Vs. 15 states two things about the large upper room:_____ &_____(6)

Christ furnishes and prepares for us a place to eat, rest and live.
First we must open our hearts and lives and then accept His preparations for us.

This upper room was also the upper room in Acts1:3 where over 100 believers met on Pentecost. And in Acts 1:12, we see the disciples, the women, the Mother of Christ and His brothers go to the upper room as they continued to pray in one accord after Christ ascension. They were staying in the upper room in Jerusalem, waiting as Jesus had directed them, until they received the power Jesus had promised.

Christ gives us the Holy Spirit. We must accept His gift.

In Acts 9:36-43 read this story and connect another death and another arising to Elisha and Elijah.

"At Joppa there was a certain disciple named Tabitha, which is translated Dorcas. This woman was full of good works and charitable deeds which she did but it happened in those days that she became sick and died. When they had washed her, they laid her in an upper room. And since Lydia was near Joppa, and the disciples had heard that Peter was there, they sent two men to him, imploring him not to delay in coming to them. Then Peter arose and went with them. When he had come, they brought him to the upper room. And all the widows stood by him weeping, showing the tunics and garments which Dorcas had made while she was with them. But Peter put them all out, and knelt down and prayed. And turning to the body he said, "Tabitha, arise."

And she opened her eyes, and when she saw Peter she sat up. Then he gave her his hand lifted her up; and when he had called the saints and widows, he presented her alive. And it became known throughout all Joppa, and many believed on the Lord."

Christ gives us life everlasting. We must accept Him to receive His gift.

Acts 20:8-12 "There were many lamps in the upper room where they were gathered together. And in a window sat a certain young man named Eutychus, who was sinking into a deep sleep. He was overcome by sleep; and as Paul continued speaking, he fell down from the third story and was taken up dead. But Paul went down, fell on him, and embracing him said, "Do not trouble yourselves, for his life is in him." Now when he had eaten, and talked a long while, even till daybreak, he departed. And they brought the young man in alive, and they were not a little comforted."

All these stories happened in the upper room. Miracle healing's.

Elijah---	Revives the widows son
Elisha...	Raises the Shunammite woman's son
Elijah...	Ahaziah falls thru the lattice and Elijah warns him 3 times that he would not leave the upper room but die. 1 Kings 1
Daniel...	Kneels and prays in the upper room –3 times
Christ...	Celebrates passover and reappears after His death.
Peter..	Raises Tabitha from the dead
Paul...	Brings Eutychus back alive from falling three story's high.

From these stories, all come from the upper room.

The Shunammite woman furnishes and prepares the upper room for Elisha.

In 2 Kings 4:10 "Please, let us make a small upper room on the wall; and let us put a bed for him there, and a table and a chair and a lamp stand; so it will be, whenever he comes to us, he can turn in there."

What are the furnishings for the room?
   7)
   8)
   9)
   10)

We will study these four elements and their significance to us as they relate to different areas in the bible. Each element will reveal much.

Pray that God will open your heart to receive the miracles that the Holy Spirit gives to us, that we will accept his truth and that we will prepare room for Him in our hearts and in our lives.

Answers:

1. **Now it happened**
2. **And it happened**
3. **Now it happened**
4. **One day**
5. **"Where is the guest room in which I may eat the Passover with My disciples?"**
6. **Furnished and prepared**
7. **Bed**
8. **Chair**
9. **Table**
10. **Lampstand**

The Bed

WEEK 3 DAY 2

We are in the Upper Room that the Shunammite woman has carefully and prayerfully "furnished and prepared" for Elisha. These two words, "furnished and prepared" are used when Jesus sends two disciples to search for the room to join His disciples together for passover.

Mark 14:13-16 "And He sent out two of his disciples and said to them, "Go into the city, and a man will meet you carrying a pitcher of water; follow him. Whenever he goes in, say to the master of the house, "The Teacher says, "Where is the guest room in which I may eat the Passover with My disciples." Then he will show you a large upper room, **furnished and prepared;** there make ready for us."

In our study we have stated that the upper room was furnished and prepared. Beth states that the nobel lady "makes room". The upper room has been built and now the Shunammite woman begins to furnish it.

The first piece of furniture is the_____1)

Look at Psalms 23 in the TMB
    "God, my shepherd!
    I do not need a thing.
    You have bedded me down in lush meadows,"
KJV: "He makes me to lie down in green pastures."

Psalm 23:2: The significance of the lush meadows or green pastures would be of concern to the sheep. They must trust their shepherd that the area of rest is safe for them to lie down. We have those same concerns when we go to rest.

What are areas of concern when you go to rest? Do you check the security of the house? Make sure the room is warm or cool?

Psalm 63:6 David worships the Lord as his every thought is on God before he sleeps.

"When I remember You on my **bed**, I meditate on You in the night watches.
Because You have been my help,
Therefore in the shadow of Your wings I will rejoice."

David is having difficulty sleeping. He directs his thoughts to God, to meditate on Him.

What are your thoughts when you are restless?

If you are in a problem sleep time or period of your life when it is difficult to sleep, then use the time wisely; do as David did. **David_____ 2) on God.**

Meditate means to speak about the thing of God or to fill one's mind with the knowledge of God. In times of sleeplessness turn to God and allow Him to fill you up and as David says; "Allow yourself to go under His wing of protection".

God is always with us, no matter where we choose to go. David speaks of a bed made in hell but God was with him.

Ps.139:8 "If I ascend into heaven, You are there; If I make my bed in hell, behold, You are there."

King Solomon speaks in the Song of Solomon of many places in his love story. The chorus calls the bride back from her daydreams and reminds her that she is Solomon's queen. Shulamite is a title. The hometown of the woman is usually thought to be Shunem. Her title sounds very much like the Hebrew pronunciation for the name Solomon. Both words are related to the Hebrew word for peace.

3)_____ is the Hebrew word for peace.

Shalom is a beautiful addition to the characteristic of the Shunammite woman. When you think of her do you think of a peaceful place? Or even that she is a peacemaker?

"Isaiah 28.20 "For the bed is too short to stretch out on, And the covering so narrow that one cannot wrap himself in it."

Have you ever been in a bed that was too short or that the covering on the bed was so narrow that you could not cover yourself?

How did you feel?

Was one of your feelings of lack of security?

"Our beds should be secure and comfortable. My Dad pulled a joke on us many times by short sheeting the bed. It was too short and we would fuss with the sheets while he laughed at our frustration." From Beth Bonner ("This is Who We Are" pg 55)

I find it hard to read these words without laughter, in a "bed that was too short and coverings so narrow". You probably have a story also, but mine is my mother's. She tells it in front of her college roommate from Furman University, who happened to be her roommate at a new teachers' home in the forties. Single women out of college who were teaching lived in a home with a supervisor. Mother and Sara Francis lived in one of these homes.

Mother would tell the story over the years, and at the end they would both laugh a contagious laugh.

They were sleeping on a double bed when mother continued to steal the covers awayand then proceeded to fanny her roommate off the bed until she was in the floor. Her crash woke Mother up.

Mother quickly sat up and said to her roommate, who was sitting in the floor, "I hope that you are happy now, you woke me up!"

Luckily these two ladies were still very close friends until my mother's death.

Share a funny bed story to the group:

Remembering childhood laughter with my girlfriends or family as we settled for the evening are great memories. I still remember the bedroom and the bed where those laughters happened. Memories that will last a lifetime.

Tomorrow we will continue to look at the bed as it relates to different areas in the scripture.

Pray for God to give you peace as you rest and to enjoy your bedroom as a place of mediation to our Lord. Allow His wings to cover you with safety and rejoice in His presence.

Answers:

1. **Bed**
2. **Mediated**
3. **Shalom**

The Bed

WEEK 3 DAY 3

In Song of Solomon 1:16 "Behold, you are handsome, my beloved! Yes pleasant! Also our bed is green."

Handsome here means fair, a word of beauty, a word not used in this generation. Once used in Biblical times and in the era before us.

Remember that great movie, "My Fair Lady?"

"The rain in Spain stays mainly in the plain!"

Solomon also refers to the bed in color. **It is**_____ **1)** .

What do you think this color means and why is this color added?:

What is another passage associated with bed and green?

2)

David finds a beautiful place for the sheep to sleep and relax in safety during the night. In Psalms 23, sleep is welcomed. The shepherd knows that he protects them. No harm can come to them. The sheep are aware of his guard. When you think of David and his provision for the sheep to rest, how do you compare what our Lord does for us in sleep?

My thoughts of bed are rest and relaxation. I can see a picture of a beautiful bed and want to crawl up and sleep. Makes me sleepy just thinking about some beds in luxury hotels. Their fluffy pillows and inviting colors make me long to jump on, curl up and sleep without any alarm or troubles in my mind. I truly believe that the Shunammite woman made the bed for Elisha one that was was inviting and welcoming.

Rest is an important function of the bed. Rest is important to God for us. He makes many provisions for us to rest. Can you think of areas that God gives or has given to us for rest:

The most obvious is our day of worship with Him. The Sabbath. It is called a day of rest. It seems this day to some is without a paying working job but full of activities. Some activities wear us out instead of helping us rest.

Ex. 31:15 "Work shall be done for six days, but the seventh is the Sabbath of rest, holy to the Lord."

The words that follow vs 15 are meaningful and need to be included:

"Whoever does any work on the Sabbath day, he shall surely be put to death. Therefore the children of Israel shall keep the Sabbath, to observe the Sabbath throughout their generations as a perpetual covenant. It is a sign between Me and the children of Israel forever; for in six days the Lord made the heavens and the earth, and on the seventh day He rested and was refreshed." vs. 16,17

These days of rest were kept in righteousness before God. Actually the Sabbath, a day of rest, is a sign. It is a reminder, it is a memorial, it is a symbol of our righteousness before God that distinguishes us from all other non- believers. This sign of "remembering the sabbath day" is one forever between God and us, His people.

What can you do to make the Sabbath day more holy for you? Do you rest?

Jesus speaks of rest in Matt. 11:29- 30 "Come to Me, all you who labor and are heavy laden, and I will give you rest. Take My yoke upon you and learn from Me, for I am gentle and lowly in heart, and you will find rest for your souls. For My yoke is easy and My burden is light."

This rest is one that we need when we are burdened or suffering under a load of responsibilities. Rest can be relief from these burdens. Jesus gives us the peace to rest in a bed of gentleness. His sincere love to us gives us peace in our heart, mind and soul; and we can rest.

Who are you when it comes to rest? Do you rest in your bed or are you restless?

Have you made your bed welcoming or is your bed cluttered and full of other things like laundry or mail that need attention?

Does a change need to occur so that when you go to bed, you rest? (Referring to the bed and its surroundings).

What can you do to make it a welcoming bed of rest?

The Shunammite woman furnished and prepared the upper room for Elisha to give him a place to rest. **When you consider the bed in this room, what do you think she added to the bed to make it welcoming to Elisha?**

When you have visitors do you have a room ready for them to make it a peaceful and restful environment?

In Isaiah, the prophet refers to the obstinate alliance with Egypt which was ill advised. The bed too short and the narrow coverings gave a false promise of security and comfort. He further states in:

Is.57:7 "On a lofty and high mountain
　　　You have set your bed;
　　　Even there you went up
　　　To offer sacrifice"

Israel has a problem with idolatry. Isaiah is pointing this out to the Israelites that they have idols but they still sacrifice in their sin. Idol worship was practiced on high mountains. Here the bed is associated with sexual aspects of idolatry. The people were easily confused between true and false worship.

How easily we can become confused with true and false worship. How easily we can have idols in our lives that take over and push God out. The phone, the internet, the tv are all examples of idols that take our time away from worshipping the King and being Kingdom workers.

Where in your life do you put idols before our Lord?

Matt 9:6 "But that you may know that the Son of Man has power on earth to forgive sins"– then He said to the paralytic, "Arise, take up your bed, and go to your house." And he arose and departed to his house."

Luke 17:34 "I tell you, in that night there will be two men in one bed: the one will be taken and the other will be left."

This scripture is speaking of the second coming and judgement.

Heb 13:4 "Marriage is honorable among all and the bed undefiled; but fornication and adulterers God will judge."

Through scripture we have seen descriptions of the bed. Fill in the blanks with these Usage words: Idolatry~ Sleep ~ Rest~ Intimacy ~ Dream

Color: 3)_____Twice-Green(Ps 23) "green pastures" referring to comfort and safety.

   4)_____Green-Song of Solomon 1:16 The bed is green referring to new life.

Position:5)____Is. 57:7 Referring to prideful
   6)_____Matt.9:6 "take up your bed" Referring to lowly, weak, vulnerable.

   7)_____Matt. 9:6 Christ gives us the stamina to boldly arise.
   8)_____Luke 17:34 Refers to being comfortable in self and then we are taken.

Pray today that God will allow you and you will allow yourself to be safe in His arms, resting in His peace.

ANSWERS:

1. Green
    Green is a meaning of new because he refers to the vineyard.
    The new grape is green.

2. Ps. 23 "He maketh me to lie down in green Pastures."

Usage: 3) Sleep
       4) Intimacy
       5) Dream
       6) Rest
       7) Intimacy
       8) Idolatry

The Bed

WEEK 3 DAY 4

The bed is one of the furnishings that the Shunammite woman has prepared for Elisha. Think of this one piece of furniture as the center piece of the room. I am sure that she made great efforts to be sure that the bed was comfortable for Elisha.

Our past days of study has seen the bed as safe, comfortable, portable, green, bold, high and lofty. Lets look today at its being shared.

In "This is Who We Are Becoming the Sons of God", Beth says "The bed can also be symbolic of a place to express love, share secrets, become intimate and spark new life! Once you have known the intimacy that comes in a trusted relationship, you realize there is no substitute.

There must be trust to have complete and total vulnerability and productive intimacy. We have so cheapened the act of intimacy between sexual partners in this culture by sharing our "bed" and exchanging intimacies with strangers with whom we do not intend to form a relationship. We waste time and energy in flirtations that lead to encounters for the express purpose of fulfilling our flesh." Beth Bonner

Paul gives us wisdom in Eph 5:23:

23) "Husbands, love your wives, just as Christ also loved the church and gave Himself for her, 26) that He might sanctify and cleanse her with the washing of water by the word, 27) that He might present her to Himself a glorious church, not having spot or wrinkle or any such thing, but that she should be holy and without blemish. 28)So husbands ought to love their own wives as their own bodies, he who loves his wife loves himself. 29) for no one ever hated his own flesh, but nourishes and cherishes it, just as the Lord does the church. 30) for we are member of His body, of His flesh and of His bones. 31) for this reason **a man shall leave his father and mother and be joined to his wife, and the two shall become one flesh.** This is a great mystery, but I speak concerning Christ and the Church. 33) Nevertheless let each one of you in particular so love his own wife as himself, and let the wife see that she respects her husband.

1) Do husbands and wife's have the same role or different?_____
2) How does our submission arise to our spouse?_____ **(vs33)**

Christ is not inferior to the Father, but is the second Person in the Trinity, so wives are equal to their own husbands.

4) When referring to the husband, is it his authority or his love?____**(vs. 23)**
5) How is this love described?_____**(vs.23)**

Paul outlines what Jesus has done for the church:

He Loved the Church so much that He was willing to suffer and die for it.
His actions saved and sanctified the church.
Jesus wanted the Church to develop into the temple of God.

Look at Gen: 2:24 "Therefore a man shall leave his father and mother and be joined to his wife, and they shall become one flesh."

Look back in Ephesians above. What verse in Ephesians is this similar to?
5)_____

Jesus refers to this text as the foundation of the biblical view of marriage.

In Matt.19:5 He refers to this verse after the Pharisees ask Him about divorce. Jesus finishes the scripture by saying in vs 5, "So, then, they are no longer two but one flesh. Therefore what God has joined together, let not man separate."

Joined together actually means "to be glued." The most permanent relationship in society is not between parent and child, but between husband and wife. If this relationship is the most permanent, then when Christ refers to His bride as the church, the church(us) has that inseparable bond. It will never go away.

The two become one flesh is the covenant of physical intimacy.

Do you see how God unites us to Him as the Bride and Groom are united?

There is no separation between God and each of us when we accept Christ as our savior. We are entwined in His love. We are inseparable.

Have you ever notice how vines grow together. Ivey and grapes grow in vines that entwine. The vines are woven between each other.

In John 15, Jesus uses the vine as an example to describe His love :

1) "I am the true vine, and My Father is the vinedresser. 2)Every branch in Me that does not bear fruit He takes away; and every branch that bears fruit He prunes, that it may bear more fruit. 3) You are already clean because of the word which I have spoken to you. 4) Abide in Me, and I in you. As the branch cannot bear fruit of itself, unless it abides in the vine, neither can you, unless you abide in Me. 5)I am the vine, you are the branches, He who abides in Me, and I in him, bears much fruit; for without Me you can do nothing."

Abiding in Christ means **to dwell, to stay, to settle in, to sink deeper and to be obedient** to Him. Choose the word in bold that most represents abide to you.

Now fill in the blank with that word below:

dwell, stay, settle in, sink deeper, be obedient to Him
"_____in me, and I in you. As the branch cannot bear fruit of itself, unless it

_____in the vine, neither can you, unless you _____in Me.
I am the vine, you are the branches, He who _____in Me, and I in him, bears much fruit; for without Me you can do nothing." 57

After reading your substituted word in the scripture above, read Ephesians 5:23-33 and relate it in your marriage.

"Husbands, love your wives, just as Christ also loved the church and gave Himself for her, that He might sanctify and cleanse her with the washing of water by the word, that He might present her to Himself a glorious church, not having spot or wrinkle or any such thing, but that she should be holy and without blemish. So husbands ought to love their own wives as their own bodies, he who loves his wife loves himself. For no one ever hated his own flesh, but nourishes and cherishes it, just as the Lord does the church. For we are member of His body, of His flesh and of His bones. **For this reason a man shall leave his father and mother and be joined to his wife, and the two shall become one flesh. This is a great mystery,** but I speak concerning Christ and the Church. Nevertheless let each one of you in particular so love his own wife as himself, and let the wife see that she respects her husband."

Do you see where a covenant relationship in marriage can be compared to a covenant relationship to Christ?

Look at vs.31 "for this reason a man shall leave his father and mother and be joined to his wife, and the two shall become one flesh. This is a great mystery, but I speak concerning Christ and the Church."

What is the great mystery?

God has revealed a mystery to us that His love is stronger than any bond of marriage. That is His covenant to us. Whether we are married, widowed, or divorced, Christ is with us and will serve as our divine partner. We should be submissive and obedient, stay in Him and dwell in Him.

The sacred secret that God reveals to us is that Christian marriage parallels the union that exists spiritually between Christ and the church.

Prayer: Seek God's guidance in your relationship with Him. Be obedient to His love for you. Abide in His love.

Answers:

1. **Different**
2. **Wife's voluntary submission arises out of her our submission to Christ**
3. **Love**
4. **Love described: Husbands are to emulate Christ's love. Love that is willing to lay down one's life for another person and serve that person even if it means suffering.**
5. **Vs 31**

What a Beautiful Bed

WEEK 3 DAY 5

In **This is Who we Are; Becoming the Sons of God**, Beth writes:

"I provide an inviting environment, one that is just as good for my husband as it is for me. I look at my bed as a cocoon. I go in tired at night and in the morning I am new. The bed is a place of rest, restoration, healing and nurture for our earthly temple. The bed I speak of now is the bed of the physical death of this body. When awaken it is a glorious spiritually mature being." Beth Bonner

The Death Bed:

Our study continues as we look at the side of the bed that would be the place where our passing to Christ might occur. In 2 Kings 4:18- 21, the Shunammite woman experiences the death of her son.

"And the child grew. Now it happened one day that he went out to his father, to the reapers. And he said to his father, 'My head, my head!'

So he said to a servant, 'Carry him to his mother.' When he had taken him and brought him to his mother, he sat on her knees till noon, and then died. And she went up and laid him on the bed of the man of God, shut the door upon him, and went out."

In 2 Kings 4:32–37

vs. 32) "When Elisha came into the house, there was the child lying dead on his bed. 33) He went in therefore, shut the door behind the two of them, and prayed to the Lord. 34) And he went up and lay on the child, and put his mouth on his mouth, his eyes on his eyes, and his hands on his hands; and he stretched himself out on the child, and the flesh of the child become warm. 35) He returned and walked back and forth in the house, and again went up and stretched himself out on him: then the child sneezed seven times, and the child opened his eyes.

36) And he called Gehazi and said, 'Call this Shunammite woman.' So he called her. And when she came in to him he said, 'Pick up your son.'

37) So she went in, fell at his feet, and bowed to the ground; then she picked up her son and went out."

Where does she lay the boy, after he has died?_____1)
**Is she full of sorrow?____2) Who gave her her son?_____3)
What do you think this says about the Shunammite woman**

What 3 things did she do: 4)*
*
*

Placing the body on the bed of the man of God also kept his death a secret until she could reach Elisha. The Shunammite woman had already seen the miracle that Elisha gave her. She knew that he was the only one she could trust.

The Shunammite woman's son has died and she places her son's body on the bed of the man that gave him life. She so believed in Elisha that she left her son in a secret place from others. She knew that the one who gave him life would also restore his life.

When she found Elisha, he asked her what was wrong, she did not panic and react in fear. Her response to Elisha "Everything is all right," seemed almost unnatural. She then would **not** leave Elisha's side until he went to Shunem.

Faith looks at situations, through God's eyes, not the eyes of our limited understanding. This woman did not panic, for she knew something more than the current circumstance.

Faith does not panic, but realizes that what looks like devastating circumstances may be God's plan to bring glory to Himself by demonstrating His power.

Some events paralyze us. Death can do that. It is always a shock. Look at the true appearance of the situation not the first. Find God in everything. Even death.

How did Elisha find the boy when he arrived?_____5)

Elisha finds the boy in Elisha's upper room, in Elisha's bed, lifeless. Elisha does several things. Look at the scripture to see what he does. 2 Kings 4:32-37:

32) "When Elisha came into the house, there was the child lying dead on his bed.

33) He went in therefore, shut the door behind the two of them, and prayed to the Lord. 34) And he went up and lay on the child, and put his mouth on his mouth, his eyes on his eyes, and his hands on his hands; and he stretched himself out on the child, and the flesh of the child become warm. 35) He returned and walked back and forth in the house, and again went up and stretched himself out on him: then the child sneezed seven times, and the child opened his eyes. 36) And he called Gehazi and said, 'Call this Shunammite woman.' So he called her. And when she came in to him he said, 'Pick up your son.' 37) So she went in, fell at his feet, and bowed to the ground; then she picked up her son and went out."

This upper room was Elisha's prayer room and he did just that, but first he closed the door behind the two of them. His actions included: **No.6)**

1)_____
2) **Sought Privacy**
3) **Lay on the child and**

The boys body became_____(7)

In vs 35, Elisha seems to take a break. He walked back and forth and then returned to the room to repeat what he had done.

Then the child sneezed. How many times?_____ (8)

Elisha sought God, who alone could grant life and perform the miraculous. The restoration of the boys life is a demonstration that life is in the hands of God.

Similarly, Elijah revived the widow's son in 1 King 17:17-24.In verse 21, Elijah stretched his body over the dead child three times. This may symbolize the power of the thrice Holy God.

Do you think that the seven times the boy sneezes symbolizes anything?

Find the Lord in your circumstance today. Exercise your faith today and trust Him for His outcome in the situation.

Prayer: Dear Father in Heaven, Thank You for Your loving hand of guidance. This is hard to do from a human standpoint (even a "child's" viewpoint), but thank You for Your chastisement. I know that You love me because You care enough to bring about or allow things to happen to stop me and redirect my priorities and my paths. When things don't turn out like I expect, it's usually because I'm not doing what You want me to do or I'm doing something that would not bring about the best results for me, my loved ones, or those in my circle of influence. I pray that You would continue to direct the work of my hands, the desires of my heart, the steps that I take, and help me to turn in trust when You redirect my paths. For God, I know that all things work together for the good of those who love You (Romans 8:28). I love You. In Jesus' name, Amen.

ANSWERS:

1. **Elisha's bed**
2. **Yes**
3. **God through Elisha**
4. **Laid him on the man of God's bed *Shut the door * Went out**
5. **Dead on his bed**
6. **Prayed: Eyes to eyes; hands to hands; mouth to mouth**
7. **Warm**
8. **Seven times**

From The Message: Nothing is impossible with God.

> *"Seek My Face, and you will find all that you have longed for.*
> *The deepest yearnings of your heart are for intimacy with Me.*
> *I know, because I designed you to desire Me. Do not feel guilty about taking time*
> *to be still in My Presence. You are simply responding to the tugs of divinity within*
> *you. I made you in My image, and I hid heaven in your heart.*
> *Your yearning for Me is a form of homesickness: longing for your true home*
> *in heaven."*

The Table

WEEK 4 DAY 1

The scripture is listed in the beginning to refresh you of our study. You can skip or reread. You will need to reference for answers to specific questions in the study.

2 Kings 4: 8–12

"Now it happened one day that Elisha went to Shunem, where there was a notable woman, and she persuaded him to eat some food. So it was, as often as he passed by, he would turn in there to eat some food. (vs.9)And she said to her husband, 'Look now, I know that this is a holy man of God, who passes by us regularly. (vs.10) Please let us make a small upper room on the wall; and let us put a bed for him there, and a table and a chair and a lampstand; so it will be, whenever he comes to us, he can turn in there.'

And it happened one day that he came there, and he turned in to the the upper room and lay down there. Then he said to Gehazi his servant, 'Call this Shunammite woman.' When he had called her, she stood before him. And he said to him, 'Say now to her, 'Look, you have been concerned for us with all this care. What can I do for you? Do you want me to speak on your behalf to the king or to the commander of the army?'

She answered, 'I dwell among my own people.'

So he said, 'What then is to be done for her?'

(vs.14)And Gehazi answered, 'Actually she has no son, and her husband is old.'

So he said, 'Call her.' When he had called her, she stood in the doorway. Then he said, 'About this time next year you shall embrace a son.'

And she said, 'No, my lord, man of God, do not lie to your maid servant!'

But the woman conceived, and bore a son when the appointed time had come, of which Elisha had told her.

And the child grew. Now it happened one day that he went out to his father, to the reapers. And he said to his father, 'My head, my head!'

So he said to a servant, 'Carry him to his mother.' When he had taken him and brought him to his mother, he sat on her knees till noon, and then died. And she went up and laid him on the bed of the man of God, shut the door upon him, and went out. Then she called to her husband, and said, 'Please send me one of the young men and one of the donkeys, that I may run to the man of God and come back.'

(vs 23)So he said, 'Why are you going to him today? It is neither the New Moon nor the Sabbath.'

And she said, 'It is well.' Then she saddled a donkey, and said to her servant, 'Drive, and go forward; do not slacken the pace for me unless I tell you.' And so she departed, and went to the man of God at Mount Carmel.

So it was, when the man of God saw her afar off, that he said to his servant Gehazi, 'Look, the Shunammite woman! Please run now to meet her, and say to her, 'Is it well with you? Is it well with your husband? Is it well with the child?'

And she answered, 'It is well.' Now when she came to the man of God at the hill, she caught him by the feet, but Gehazi came near to her to push her away. But the man of God said, 'Let her alone; for her soul is in deep distress, and the Lord has hidden it from me, and has not told me.'

So she said, 'Did I ask a son of my lord? Did I not say, 'Do not deceive me?'

Then he said to Gehazi, 'Get yourself ready, and take my staff in your hand, and be on your way. If you meet anyone, do not greet him; and if anyone greets you, do not answer him: but lay my staff on the face of the child.'

And the mother of the child said, 'As the Lord lives, and as your soul lives, I will not leave you.' So he arose and followed her. Now Gehazi went on ahead of them, and laid the staff on the face of the child; but there was neither voice nor hearing. Therefore he went back to meet him, and told him, saying, 'The child has not awakened.'

When Elisha came into the house, there was the child, lying dead on his bed. He went in therefore, shut the door behind the two of them, and prayed to the Lord. And he went up and lay on the child, and put his mouth on his mouth, his eyes on his eyes, and his hands on his hands; and he stretched himself out on the child, and the flesh of the child became warm. He returned and walked back and forth in the house, and again went up and stretched himself out on him; then the child sneezed seven times and the child opened his eyes. And he called Gehazi and said, 'Call this Shunammite woman.' So he called her. And when she came into him, he said. 'Pick up your son.' So she went in, fell at his feet, and bowed to the ground; then she picked up her son and went out."

Last week we studied one of the elements in the room that the Shunammite woman had carefully prepared for Elisha. It was the bed. Today we will look at the table. It seems insignificant but all the elements are important.

Today we will look at the Biblical reference about the table. Tomorrow we will look more on a personal level, looking at how we should organize our personal table.

When you think of a table in the Bible, what comes to your mind?

These were mine:
> The Lord's Table;
> In Ps 23–table prepared before us; and
> The tables that Jesus turned at the temple(Matt 21:12).

In Acts 6:2 "Then the twelve summoned the multitude of the disciple and said, "It is not desirable that we should leave the word of God and serve tables. 3)Therefore, brethren, seek out from among you seven of good reputation, full of the Holy Spirit and wisdom, whom we may appoint over this business; 4)but we will give ourselves continually to prayer and to the ministry of the word."

These scriptures are the first appointing of deacons. In Old and New Testament times, business was transacted at a table. You did not sit at a table with someone unless you were in agreement with them or you aimed to make an agreement with them.

Jesus was criticized for eating with sinners. He sat at the same table with them.

The first table we see is in Exodus is the Table of Showbread. God in great detail describes the building of this table. Listen to the words of the table that will reside in the tabernacle:

"You shall also make a table of acacia wood; two cubits shall be its length, A cubit its width, and a cubit and a half its height. And you shall overlay it with pure gold, and make a molding of gold all around. You shall make for it a frame of a handbreadth all around and you shall make a gold (64) molding for the frame all around. And you shall make for it four rings of gold and put the rings on the four corners that are at its four legs. The rings shall be close to the frame, as holders for the poles to bear the table. And you shall make the poles of acacia wood, and overlay them with gold, that the table may be carried with them. You shall make its dishes, its pans, its pitchers, and its bowls for pouring. You shall make them of pure gold. And you shall set the showbread on the table before Me always."

What a beautiful table. Why such a fuss about a table?

The table used to display 12 loaves of bread in the presence of the Lord was approximately 3 feet long, 18 inches wide, and 27 inches high.

The gold overlay is the same as in the Ark of the Covenant. The rings were for properly transporting and the poles protected the holy object from human hands. Everything was in honor of physically representing the holiness.

The twelve loaves represent the twelve tribes of Israel. They are called showbread because it was placed symbolically before the "face" of God.

This table, the Table of Showbread, was kept in the tabernacle where also was the Ark of the Covenant. The tabernacle was to provide a place where God might dwell among his people.

In Psalms 23:5 "You prepare a table before me in the presence of my enemies;" This verse hastens thoughts of a banquet feast. All luxury.

The Shunammite woman was one that would have prepared a beautiful table that meet all of Elisha's needs.

The Israelites were rebellious to God, but in His kindness He gave them food in the wilderness. They even questioned His authority to do so in Psalms:

Ps 78:19 "Yes, they spoke against God: They said, "Can God prepare a table in the wilderness?"

What is the emotion that you feel in reading this verse:
    toward the Israelites:
    toward God:

Do you encounter these same questions when you believe the impossible could never happen, that God would never provide for you?

How do you manifest these feelings toward yourself and toward God?

Matt 26:6-7 "And when Jesus was in Bethany at the house of Simon the leper, a woman came to Him having an alabaster flask of very costly fragrant oil, and she poured it on his head as He sat at the table."

Where is Jesus?_____1)
Who is he sitting with?_____2)
What was Mary(the woman) doing?_____3)

This anointing is days prior to the Passover. Jesus sees the pouring of the fragrant oil on His body as an anticipation of His death. Normally, oils are used after death.

In the scripture above, after Jesus' anointing, is the celebration of the Passover. It is also called the first day of the Feast of the Unleavened Bread. Jesus sits in the upper room with His disciples and teaches them a celebration of Him that is meaningful to us today.

It is_____ 4)

The Lord's Supper is a meaningful celebration to the Christian today. It can be related to the Past, Present and Future.

Past: Time of Remembrance and the Eucharist
    Luke 22:19 "And Jesus took bread, gave thanks and broke it and gave it to them saying, 'This is My body which is given for you; do this in remembrance of Me.'"

What are the words Jesus uses about the taking of the bread? 5)

The Eucharist is to be an occasion for expressing out deepest praise and appreciation for all Jesus Christ has done for us.

Jewish passover meal proclaims– Hebrew's deliverance from bondage. Christians proclaim in The Lord's Supper–deliverance from sin.

Present: The Lord's Supper becomes a time of refreshing and communion. As we participate in communion, we participate in the benefits of Jesus' death and of Jesus' resurrection life. By doing this we become nourished and empowered from the risen Christ through the Spirit.

Future: The Lord's Supper becomes a time of anticipation. We renew our dedication to Christ. We renew our dedication to other Christians. This time is one of hope in anticipation of His coming. After His return we shall partake with Him.

Matt 26:29 "But I say to you, I will not drink of this fruit of the vine from now on until that day when I drink it new with you in My Father's Kingdom."

I love that Christ will drink with us in His Father's Kingdom. We will share time with Him.

The Bible does not tell us how often to observe The Lord's Supper, the Eucharist. John Wesley speaks of the strengthening of his participation and his guidelines were as often as you can.

Do you feel the strengthening of Christ when you take communion?
What does the word communion mean?

What does the taking of communion mean to you?

Matt 26:26-29 "And as they were eating, Jesus took bread, blessed and broke it and gave it to the disciples and said, 'Take and eat; this is My body.'"

Then He took the cup, and gave thanks, and gave it to them, saying, 'Drink from it, all of you. For this is My blood of the new covenant, which is shed for many for the remission of sins. But I say to you, I will not drink of this fruit of the vine from now on until that day when I drink it new with you in My Father's Kingdom.'"

Prayer: Lord lead us to your table in reverence of who You are, remembering the sacrifice You made for us. Our prayer is for Your strength daily that Christ gives us by asking for forgiveness of sin, communion with Him and by the renewing of His Spirit within us. Even though we are sinners, You eat at the table with us and accept who we are.

Answers:

1. **Jesus is in Bethany**
2. **Jesus is sitting with Simon, the leper**
3. **She is anointing Him for burial**
4. **The Lord's Supper**
5. **Do this in remembrance of me**

The Table

WEEK 4 DAY 2

Yesterday we looked at the table as a place to eat and to fellowship. We also saw the Lord's Table as seen in the Holy of Holies. We saw in the New Testament the table is the communion table where we rededicate ourselves to Christ.

Today we will look at the table as a place that we would call our desk. The desk where we plan, write and organize. This area is the heart of "This is Who We Are". It helps you establish with the Lord a plan to become spiritually beautiful.

What are your thoughts of the perfect desk? Close your eyes....think of it....there it is....now, write it down:

Mine is a small desk with 2 drawers, 4 cubicles, a comfortable chair with a side area of baskets for my books and files. It is overlooking the sea. Warm colors in the room with pictures of the children, grandchildren, family and friends. Not there yet, but I can see it! It actually looks over the back yard, a sea of leaves. Still beautiful.

Two scriptures are in front of me on the desk so that I see them everyday–Yours will be your favorite. These are mine:

Jeremiah 29:11 "For I know the thoughts that I think toward you, says the Lord, thoughts of peace and not of evil, to give you a future and a hope."

Matt. 6:33 & 34 "Seek you first the kingdom of God and His righteousness, and all these things shall be added to you. Therefore do not worry about tomorrow, for tomorrow will worry about its own things. Sufficient for the day is its own trouble."

What is your favorite life verse that you would keep near?

With all of our electronics keeping track of our lives, it is easy to walk away from some of the planning skills that have been successful in the past. A notebook will help you get back on track. Notebook planning written or on your computer will help you get organized. Help you keep Christ the center of your life.

This is your NOTEBOOK: This is who you are.....

Purchase your notebook that has a week at a glance with a quick turn to month at a glance. Pray over your purchase and then pray for your planning time, your week and your month. Ask for God's guidance.

Choose a day that weekly has the least activities. Use this day to plan your week, month or year. A day that is a quiet and without interruption is best. Make it a time that worries are minimal.

Begin your notebook. It does not have to be January. You can start anytime. But get started. Are you excited? I am for you.

    Record known appointments or specific daily activities.
    Record birthdays or other special events.

Weekly:

    Begin with prayer– God will guide you to make powerful decisions.
    Each day should hold your daily schedule and other activities.
    Place in travel times. It takes 30 min to get to work? Put it in your planner.
    Write in preparation times. How many minutes to dress
    Make categories: To call; To email; To write; written on each day to remind
        you of communications.
    Plan the best Bible study/prayer time for each day, record in planner.
        Be realistic.
    Attach a paperclip to hold laundry slips or receipts that you need to return
        or record.
    When do you work out?   Record it
    Do you travel?   Be sure to record flights, travel time etc.

Daily:

Begin your day with prayer as you wake up.

First page of your calendar should appear before you or marked with a book mark for quick reference.

Look at your day calendar to confirm when/ where you need to be.

Follow your schedule being flexible to change but aware of interferences.

Keep your book with you at all times to drop notes in on specific days to do. Better than sticky notes all over the house.

If someone ask you a date or a time to do something your calendar will be in front of you to make that decision to go or not.

Someone ask to borrow something: Note to take it to them, note that they borrowed & note of return date. How many books or objects have you borrowed or let someone borrow and the return has not or never will happen.

Medications are recorded when and time to take. I have a friend who had a kidney transplant who takes over 20 medications. I cannot remember if I took my one much less 20. Then when you go to the Dr., you have your list in front of you for what is needed to reorder and/or problems.

Include naps if you are a napper. Knowing a nap is part of your plan will allow you to let go of everything, shut down and take a good nap.

When you remember an item you need from the store, write it on the day that you go to the grocery store and bam,...it is in front of you, no longer forgotten. (If your notebook is a smaller size and easy to tote in grocery then write it on the page; if not then write on a sticky for the day you go- Your list will always be with you.)

You can do directions this same way. Write them on a sticky, place in your notebook on the day you are going. On the day you go, stick the directions on the dashboard so it is directly in front of you. After used, place them in the back of your notebook under that person's contact information. You will never ask for that direction again. GPS has taken care of this problem, but somedays, we still need written directions.

At the End of the day:

Review your day. Move things not done to another day or forget.

Clean out your purse daily recording receipts, etc.

Thank the Lord for all HE has done.

Go over tomorrows agenda preparing in prayer your agenda.

Take a quick glance at week/next week- tweet-as needed.

What do you need for tomorrow- pile it at door- ready to go.

PRAY over people you have seen/people you will see.
You are going to sleep better and wake up refreshed.
Read today. What have you done & what you will do.
Read tomorrow- Do clothes need to be prepared? etc

Quarterly:

Clean out closets and drawers according to the change of season.
Plan one full day with the Lord in prayer and Bible study or a special event.
Make date nights with loved ones or someone who needs help.
"To DO"–Like or Dislike but need to do and/or I hate to do but got to do.
Record "to do's" on days to be completed. Then hate "to do's" on different days.
Spread them out.
Make sure you record them when they are to be done in your notebook.
When you deliberately plan "to do" those hated task, you are more apt "to do" them.
Accomplished! You have overcome the habit of procrastination.
Quiet Accomplishment! (Woohoo!! Dancing in the street)

Let's Get Real

Make God the Center of your Life- No matter what else- Make time for Him.
Times may vary, but adjust daily until you find what works.
Always look ahead- (If you were driving you would be prepared for what's next- you look ahead in anticipation).
Cross off items as you go- So fun to accomplish things to do!

Your notebook will not be identical to anyone but you. It will reflect
Who You Are.

"Make your desk your own, but make it a tool to help you live a life of obedience to God and effectiveness to people." Anne Ortlund.

In your notebook make a Goal section. God does have goals for you. You write your own in prayer:

Life Goals:

Spiritual Goals-ask God -He will tell you.
With yourself- Who you want to be.

Your money– Small goals that turn into large ones.
Love ones– how you interact with them.
Friends– growing and developing.
Work– where are you going in your work?
Hobbies & Play– dreams of things you want to do.
Living Quarters– decorating, etc.
Clothing– building ideals.
Workout Goals.

Goals should be as measurable as possible.

Before you go shopping, clean out your closet, your fridge, your cabinets. You might be surprised that you already have what you wrote to purchase.

Goal writing takes time and much prayer. Include your goals at the top of your monthly calendar. Or one big goal so that you can concentrate on it. Here are my March goals that I wrote:

Follow God radically and only God.
Increase my tithe to 15% and joyfully give more.
Recklessly give more time to prayer than before.
Lead family to God every day.
Pray for my grandchildren the perfect mate and their children to come.
Be thankful for everything even my suffering.
Stand firm in the faith–– Jesus is coming soon!

In 1976, my goal was to mentor 100 women to know Jesus as their personal Lord or help them after they had been saved. God continues to lead me to women who need that one word that He tells me for them to accept Him and help them continue on His path.

Tomorrow we will continue more about the desk and, specifically, your notebook.

Prayer: God direct our path to using a notebook to help You increase in our life. Help us to allow You to be our center and grow in Your word, touching others to see Your light shine through us.

The Table
Your Desk/Your Notebook

WEEK 4 DAY 3

Yesterday we looked at the Desk and making your notebook work for you in the section of daily, weekly, and monthly living. We also looked at setting goals.

Let us start with another section of your notebook today. If we are to become the daughters of God, this section should become a large part of our lives. It is BIble Study.

Bible Study: One of the best ways to organize your bible study section is by having your file cabinet sectioned by the books of the bible, Old to New Testament–Genesis to Revelation. For more, put a sheet in the back of your file cabinet for references such as The Shunammite Woman or David or Categories such as love, hope, and patience. Leave your current study with you at all times, and then, as you finish, drop them into your file folders. "H" for Hope. "L" for Love. After you make your notes or after that series is finished, then drop them into the file cabinet. You will only have what is current and you can reference back to what is needed in the files.

Begin making notes and refreshen them if time allows. Go back and read as you find time or review these notes when you are studying that scripture or that theme. Pray before you begin asking God for guidance. He will guide you.

Oh, and He will bless you with His word! Read Revelation 1. God blesses the reader of The Word and the hearer of The Word.

Disciples: Next section of your notebook:

Do you remember the Great Commission? Write it in your own words:

Matt 28:18-20 "And Jesus came and spoke to them saying, 'All authority has been given to Me in heaven and on earth. 19) Go therefore and make disciples of all the nations, baptizing them in the name of the Father and of the Son and of the Holy Spirit, teaching them to observe all things that I have commanded you; and lo, I am with you always, even to the end of the age. Amen.'"

Because Jesus has authority we all need to hear His gospel.

WHO do you think needs to hear the gospel?

Christ ask _____ **1)**

What are the three things Christ ask us to do when we are making disciples: (answer #2)
1.
2.
3.

So how are you achieving the Great Commission?

The last words Jesus spoke in this scripture were:

"I am with you always."

These words give me cold chills, literally down my spine because I know that He is with me in everything I do. These words demonstrate that Jesus is the true Immanuel, "God with us".

Matt 1:23 "Behold, the virgin shall be with child, and bear a Son, and they shall call His name Immanuel, which is translated, 'God with us.'"

Discples: This section would contain your Bible study group, people you are witnessing to and new Christians that need discipleship. Your notebook section called disciples may have different areas of calling:

People who need to know Christ: witness to them- pray for God to show you the words that the Holy Spirit will give you.
People who know Christ: Pray and encourage them.

People who need to know more about Christ: New Christians who need to know more of what God has taught you.

Follow up calls, meetings and accountability are in the discipleship section. Listed below are "13 ways to love your neighbor". These are all in the New Testament, and they show how members of the Body of Christ can communicate with other members of the Body of Christ. Write beside each one a scripture that corresponds:

Suffering Together
Rejoicing Together
Bearing one another's burdens
Restoring one another
Praying together
Teaching admonishing
Refreshing one another
Encouraging one another
Forgiving one another
Confessing to one another
Being Truthful with one another
Stimulating one another
Giving to one another

Share with your group one of your scripture references.
Share your scripture reference with me. janevanlaar@yahoo.com

Write names of people that need specific areas of the thirteen above discipleships to encourage them in that specific need. Write the name beside the list or make a list on a separate page. Begin to pray for the person and the specific request.

Friends and Family:Your Notebook would also contain a section for your little ones, family and friends.

Children
Grandchildren
Parents
Friends
Neighbors

Let the words flow in these sections.

*Cute things the children say

   Words of encouragement to and from others.
   Notes from friends

I have notebooks back to 1976 and the entertainment is endless with words recorded that my son said when he was a little one, his growing up, and now new ones from his children. You do not want to forget those cute sayings they have.

Countless prayers have gone up for my neighbors, friends and family who have not known Christ. Illness or surgeries and general blessings are recorded in this section.

Currently prayers are for my son and his precious wife, each grandchild, their spouses to-be, their children, my great- grandchildren and their spouses and children, my great great- grandchildren and their spouses and children, and my great, great, great- grandchildren and their spouses and children. Five generations of children who I pray will accept Christ first, have Christian spouses and raise Christian children. I tell my grandchildren that I pray for their spouse and their children and their grandchildren. Kindly they respond with, "Thank you, Gram!" (Maybe a question mark from them instead.)

In the early nineties my neighborhood was a new community, and my yard was in a great need of love. Each plant planted was named for after a neighbor. As I would water or fuss over that plant, I would pray for the soul or the need of that neighbor.

One neighbor would continually tell me how beautiful the plant I named after her was. She never knew I had named that plant for her.

One day she came and told me they were moving.

That day, I dug up the plant and gave it to her and told her that Jesus loved her. Just like that plant, He nourishes her, cares about her and helps her to grow. Many sacrifices were made to make sure that plant survived and grew. Jesus loved her so much that He died for her sins and if she accepts Him in her heart as her Savior, then He will give her eternal life. She took the plant. If she accepted Christ that day or after, she did not tell me. I continue to pray for her. Christ gives us a choice. He gave me the ability to plant the seed.

Sermons: This section includes all teachings and preaching. Make notes of scripture and quick phrases. Transfer these notes into your Bible files after you have read again. If you pick up an audio tape, put the two together. There is such enjoyment of reading old notes from pastors remembered.

Sermon notes that I started date back to 1968 when I made a public announcement of my faith. These are hard to read but are a wonderful memory for me. My father informed me that since I had ants in my pants in church and that I like to write notes to my girlfriends then I could write the sermon notes and read them back to him. He thought it was punishment but I grew and learned from all those notes. It was an inspiration.

Honestly, I believe that pastors like for us to take notes.

What do you think?

Prayers: Write prayers in the back of your notebook.

Do you write your prayers? Take a moment to write one now. It is challenging if you have never done so, but wait for that wonderful spirit to send cold chills down your spine.

Let the words flow like you are talking. Go back when we finish the study and see how God takes every prayer seriously.

Tell Father God that you love Him. Write it down and see what a wonderful feeling that He gives you for expressing your love for Him. "I love you, Father!"

When you look back you will see God's answers to your prayers, your moods, His love, your joy, His encouragement and adoration for you. Sometimes there's great joy that He said "No" and greater joy when He says "Yes"!

Take your notebook everywhere. Not only are you doing a calendar but you are praying for others, recording thoughts and making quick reminders for the brain. How many times do you sit waiting and wish you had something inspirational to read, study or say a prayer for someone?

If you notebook is on the seat of the car when you are at a stop light, then you can reach over and flip to prayer request and say a prayer for someone or pray about a goal that you have recorded.

Anne Ortlund writes in her book "Disciples of A Beautiful Woman".

"Your notebook is filled with that which is most meaningful in every area of your total life, and as you learn to use it continuously through each day, you will.

Stay on target in your living
Become more prayerful
Be more deeply impressed by God's truths
Keep your mind filled with the pure, the beautiful
Not forget what you are supposed to do."

Anne continues, 'All through the years I had fleeting thoughts of wonderful things to be or do. Or I had moments of actual conviction that I really ought to be this or do that. But somehow I let the moment pass. Now the pressure is on my notebook, it tells me 'You are going to meet the Lord first, and you are going to meet him now.'"

Prayer: Lord, God our Father, we earnestly give You our love and adoration. You have inspired us to read these words. Now let us put them into action so that we might grow deeper in You and with others. Amen

Answers:

Everyone needs to hear about Christ

1. **People who know Christ**
2. **Go or Pray**
   Encourage or Baptize
   Teach or Witness

The Table

WEEK 4 DAY 4

In writing, I thought the table would take one day but it has covered more. References–will now mostly be from Beth's book, "This Is Who We Are; How We Become The Sons of God."

The table is significant to the understanding of how God communes with us. The table represents the following:

It holds our nourishment and nutrients.
It is a place of fellowship–exchanging thoughts, visions and expressions.
It is a place to sit and write what comes from within our hearts.
It is an act of trust to share a table.
It is an act of intimacy.
It is the place for The Lord's Supper.

You will look at a table differently now instead of just a piece of furniture.

The brotherhood of disciples who were with Jesus shared a table with him on their private teaching sessions as this was a time to let down their guard and truly relax. Today families gather around tables and share stories, information and laughter.

The last supper with Jesus led to more than just full stomachs and relaxed conversation. Jesus took the time to reveal Himself as the Savior who would lay down His life.

Jesus broke the bread and served the wine purposefully. Two thousand years later, we gather to do the same to remember He is the bread of life and He shed blood for our sins.

Transubstantiation is the belief that the bread and wine become the real Body of Christ once they are blessed. Others celebrate the Lord's supper as a communion in a symbolic gesture. Each method is employed to accomplish the presence of our Lord in obedience to Him.

Ps 23:5 in The Message says: "You serve me a six-course dinner right in front of my enemies. You revive my drooping head; my cup brims with blessing."

What do these words mean to you:

God does not just provide: He provides more at that moment when we are in the middle of great hardship, fighting with the enemy within or without. God is there to provide the sustenance we need to survive and more.

At the Table of Communion we need_____. 1)
At the table of life we need_____. 2)

At each table we need God where He provides for us. We starve physically and spiritually without Him, becoming incapable of being of use to Him.

At The Lord's Supper Jesus reveals Himself as the Savior. Judas is exposed and Peter has a blatant outburst of protest. The Disciples then argue over Who is the Greatest in Luke 22: 24-30. Underline serve and table as you read:

"Now there was also a dispute among them, as to which of them should be considered the greatest. 25) And He said to them, 'The Kings of the Gentiles exercise lordship over them, and those who exercise authority over them are called benefactors. 26) But not so among you; on the contrary, he who is greatest among you, let him be as the younger, and he who governs as he who serves. 27) For who is greater, he who sits at the table, or he who serves? Is it not he who sits at the table? Yet I am among you as the One who serves.'

28) 'But you are those who have continued with Me in My trials. 29) And I bestow upon you a kingdom, just as My Father bestowed one upon Me, that you may eat and drink at My table in My kingdom, and sit on thrones judging the twelve tribes of Israel.'"

From the above scripture: Who is greater in God's Kingdom, the one who sits or the one who serves?

Did Christ sit or serve?

Who gave Christ His Kingdom?

The disciples of Christ will sit at His table and do these things:
*
*
*

True leaders labor for others, as a servant would. Leadership in the church does not exalt; it serves.

Describe the Lord's view of greatness:

The disciples had been present and had suffered with Him during Jesus' ministry. He passed His kingdom authority to them. They will plant churches as part of Christ kingdom.

Their promise of future blessing and authority will be that they will sit at the banquet of victory and have the right to help Jesus rule over Israel on His return.

Matt. 19:28 "So Jesus said to them 'Assuredly I say to you that in the regeneration, when the Son of Man sits on the throne of His glory, you who have followed Me will also sit on twelve thrones, judging the twelve tribes of Israel.'"

2 Tim 2 :11–13
> "This is a faithful saying:
> For if we died with Him,
>   We shall also live with Him.
> For if we endure,
>   We shall also reign with Him.
> For if we deny Him,
>   He also will deny us,
> For if we are faithless.
>   He remains faithful;
>   He cannot deny Himself.

Prayer: Lord, as we gather at the table to celebrate your life, give us the patience to endure as you did and to serve others humbly. Amen

ANSWERS:

1. God
2. God
3. The one who serves.
4. Christ served
5. His Father
6. Eat, Drink, Judge

The Table

WEEK 4 DAY 5

"Table Teamwork" from "This is Who We Are; Becoming the Sons of God," by Beth Bonner.

Look at 2 Samuel 9. David is seeking out anyone left in Saul's house to show kindness to Jonathan. Mephibosheth, Jonathan's lame son, has been revealed by Ziba, a servant. David sends for him.

2 Samuel 9:7

"So David said to him, 'Do not fear, for I will surely show you kindness for Jonathan, your father's sake, and will restore to you all the land of Saul, your Grandfather: and you shall eat bread at my table continually.'"

Who is Mephibosheth?_____1)
How is he afflicted?_____2)

To eat bread at the king's table was not a temporary honor; it meant that he would have a pension from the king. David granted throughout Mephibosheth's life the privilege to eat at his table.

Can we honor that God does the same for us? He ask us to eat at His table. He lets us know that we are welcomed and that we can stay forever.

This act of kindness is God's grace. Mephibosheth did nothing to deserve this wonderful blessing but God granted him blessings. That is grace. We are His sons and daughters, and God blesses believers likewise– not because of good work, but because of God's faithfulness to the new covenant and the promises of the gospel. It is because of His grace.

Eph. 2:8-9 "For by you have been saved through, and that not of yourselves; it is the gift of God, not of works, lest anyone should boast."

Grace means receiving something you do not deserve.
That is God's grace.

Fill in the blanks with the word ~Covenant~
Jerm 31:31–34 A New Covenant

"Behold the days are coming, says the Lord, when I will make a new_____
with the house of Israel and with the house of Judah---32) not according to
the_____ that I made with their fathers in the day that I took them by
the hand to lead them out of the land of Egypt, My_____ which they
broke though I was a husband to them, says the Lord. 33) But this is the
_____ that I will make with the house of Israel after those days, says
the Lord: I will put My law in their minds, and write it on their hearts; and I
will be their God, and they shall be My people. 34) No more shall every man
teach his neighbor, and every man his brother, saying, Know the Lord, for
they all shall know Me, from the least of them to the greatest of them, says
the Lord For I will forgive their iniquity, and their sin I will remember no
more."

We are the sons of God.....
John 1:12 "But as many as received Him, to them He gave the right to become
children of God, to those who believe in His name."

What do you think 'believe in His name' mean's?_____4)

Write Names of God you know:5)

Do you believe in His Name?
He gave the right for us to become the_____ 6)
What is the only thing we have to do to become a member of God's family?
7)

Romans 8:15 "For you did not receive the spirit of bondage again to fear, but
you received the Spirit of adoption by whom we cry out, 'Abba Father.'"

What in this text is different about the 'spirit of bondage' to the 'Spirit of
adoption'?_____ 8)

Eph 1:4–5 "He chose us in Him before the foundation of the world, that we
should be holy and without blame before Him in love, having predestined us to
adoption as sons by Jesus Christ to Himself, according to the good pleasure of
His will."

Remember Zacchaeus, the tax collector, a simple man, short in stature that wanted to position himself for a better view of Jesus. He is noticed and Jesus ask to eat at his table and stay with him in Mark 2:17.

Another tax collector, Levi, whom Jesus found sitting at the tax collecting table, was asked to "Follow Me". Levi gave Him a great feast in his own house. The guests were other tax collectors which caused the Pharisees to complain and ask, "Why do you eat and drink with tax collectors and sinners?"

Jesus answered, "Those who are well have no need of a physician, but those who are sick. I did not come to call the righteous, but sinners, to repentance."

Jesus used the table to express the love and the acceptance these people had never felt. This expression was to His followers who He wants at His table. Not the religious. Not the highly educated. But those with the most need.

Prayer: Oh Lord let us spread the table and open our eyes to the needy. Let us share and expect nothing in return. These also are your sons and daughters looking for an open door. Let us invite everyone to partake of Your goodness. Let us be an example of Christ. Thank You for allowing us to be Your people and the object of Your love. Amen

ANSWERS:

1. Jonathan's son; Saul's grandson
2. Lame foot
3. Grace, faith
4. Lord of Salvation
5. The Word, the Life, the Light, the Christ, the Son of God, Jesus
6. Children of God
7. Believe
8. Christ– notice the S is capitalized in Spirit.

God Revealed

As I walked out onto the sixth floor of my condo, which is the outside doggie walk heading east, the sun nearly blinded me with its brightness. Instead of closing my eyes tight, I gently closed my eyes and held my head back absorbing the sun into myself. Walking with eyes shut and head back I tried to stay on the path.

I continued walking.... slowly on the path, breathing in the warm air, allowing the sun to melt into my face, I realized that it was actually brighter than I had ever felt before. I tried to open my eyes but the intensity was more than my eyes would allow.

I cracked a quarter of an eye but the light hit me hard like I was walking on a lighted stage. I thought my next step would be directly onto the sun. The brightness was all I saw. Nothing to the right or left just intense brightness.

As I walked, I remembered that I had prayed before going out of the door, "God reveal Yourself to me in some visible way."

I had an automatic feeling of joy as I realized I felt God all around me. The scripture from Revelation 1:16 burst in my head, ".....and His face shone like the power of the sun in unclouded brilliance."

I wanted to dance. That great feeling and excitement of dancing, like the song.."dancing in the street" that always makes me want to jump out of my car and dance, flooded my thoughts. The dance I felt was the sun dancing around me. Great feelings of happiness were in me as each ray bounced its way around my body. It was warm and inviting. I felt its warmth on my face and arms.

Did I see Him?
I believe that God tells us that He is all around. Allowing Him to touch us through His love and His kindness takes a willingness of our heart, mind and strength. He gives us much more!
Revelation 1:17 "When I saw Him, I fell at His feet as if I were dead; but He laid His right hand on me and said "Don't be afraid....."

I want to KNOW HIM! I want to know everything about Him!
Do you? Do you want to know everything about God? Do you want to take a journey to allow Him to reveal himself to you? Open your heart, hear His voice, allow Him to love you.

"He reached down from heaven and took me and drew me out of great trials. He rescued me from deep waters." Psalms 18:16.

" 'My Father will love you and I will too, and I will reveal Myself to you' Jesus spoke." John 14:21

The Chair

WEEK 5 DAY 1

This week we look at another element of the room that the Shunammite woman has prepared for the prophet Elisha. The chair seems necessary but a small element of the room.

Let's first look into the book "This is Who We Are: Becoming the sons of God", as Beth Speaks on Page 131.

A refreshing thought:....

Chapter 21
"SIT DOWN AND SET A SPELL"

"I don't really know why my grandparents generation used this saying, but I remember it. Do you? It always made me feel good to hear someone say these words.

I was raised in the south, and we loved to sit outside on a porch swing, drink sweet iced tea, and have idle conversation with friends and family. If someone knew you well, they would invite you up to sit with them. Sweet iced tea and sweets were served. There was no better feeling than sitting with someone sharing. You were investing your time in them and they were investing time in you.

Our generation is Facebook. Theirs was time: "Sit down and set a spell". The people of the older generation sat in front of each other, willing to invest time with each other." Beth Bonner

A chair says that I want you to sit down. This woman had prepared a place for Elisha to get off his feet. Its place is making room for God to come into your life.

In the Bible, the chair symbolizes a place to hold God's glory. It is indicative of royalty such as we find with a throne. The word "footstool" is biblically interchangeable with "chair". Chair – Footstool is also used to denote authority:

"Heaven is His throne and earth is His footstool." The footstool is a place to bow at His feet and worship. It holds the weight and the glory.

"Exalt the Lord our God, and worship at His footstool–He is holy."
Psalm 95:5

The Shunammite woman was expectant of the anointing of the man of God. She was eager to be in the presence of God in the form of His prophet. She was indicating that she totally expected the glory of God to be resting in that room of sacrifice!

God's glory means weightiness or His fullness.

How do you provide a chair for His glory?

Do you sit with God when He says to you, "Sit down and set a while"?

Ps 47:8 "God reigns over the nations; God sits on His holy throne."

Do you believe that God is King over all the earth?

Is 40:22 "It is He who sits above the circle of the earth, ..."

The Shunammite woman has prepared for Elisha a chair for his room.

Picture the chair in your thoughts and write your thought:

Visiting many historical places in my youth always took me through the home of famous people. An emphasis seemed to be placed on the bedrooms. The desk and chair in each room had special notations because that was where the famous person had written or had otherwise created life's great accomplishments.

Where does God sit?_____**1)**

In Is 40:22 the words are, "It is He who sits above the circle of the earth..."

Ps 25:8 "...God sits on His holy throne."
Rev. 4:9 "Him who sits on the throne, who lives forever and ever."
Matt 19:28 "Jesus, the Son of Man, sits on the throne of His glory,...."

1 King 22:19 "Then Micah (the prophet) said, Therefore hear the word of the Lord; I saw the Lord sitting on His throne...."

These words are repeated in 2 Chr. 18:18 "Then Micah said, "Therefore hear the word of the Lord I saw the Lord sitting on His throne,..."

Where does the Lord sit?_____2)

We see God's sovereignty over all as He sits on his throne above the earth.

In Dan 7:13,14 "Christ is today seated at the right hand of the eternal throne of the Father."

Where does Christ sit?_____3)

In Rev 3:21 "To him who overcomes I will grant to sit with Me on My throne as I also overcame and sat down with my Father on His throne."

Revelation affirms God's sovereign control over history and the certainty of His plan for the future. It reminds us that our present difficulties have a connection to the future firmly in God's hands.

Refer to Rev. 3:21 "To him who overcomes I will grant to sit with Me on My throne as I also overcame and sat down with my Father on His throne."

Who is the Me and My on the throne?_____4)
Who is the Father and His?_____5)
Who is him?_____6)
What is granted?_____7)

Jesus overcame, we must overcome. Do you see that Jesus helps us overcome then we sit with Jesus.

Prayer: Thank you for the promise to us as faithful Christians, that when we overcome as believers, we will share the actual throne with Christ. Help us to overcome by being like you and following your example by being humbly obedient. Help us to persevere in faith despite the suffering. Amen.

Answers:

1. **On His holy throne: above the circle of the earth**
2. **Sitting on His throne**
3. **"Christ is today seated at the right hand of the eternal throne of the Father."**
4. **Jesus**
5. **God**
6. **Us**
7. **To sit with Jesus**

Prayer: As we go through these final weeks, Lord, we worship you knowing that you are King of Kings and Lord of Lords. Write on our hearts the love that only you can give us. Let us be aware that you reign. Let us sit at your throne of glory and worship you. Amen.

The Chair

WEEK 5 DAY 2

In Knoxville, TN, Beth Moore announced on stage how she was so thankful to a choir that had assembled. Their singing was amazing at her weekend event. Beth was praying while the choir was practicing the night before, when a choir member quietly approached her. He kindly said that he did not want to interfere with her time. He asked if he and some men could pray over the seats on Friday, during the day, before the women arrived on Friday evening.

Feeling blessed, she called the security in the Knoxville arena to give permission to allow these men to come in with passes to pray over the seats.

Friday morning arrived and Beth received a call from the security of the building. "Mrs. Moore".

"Yes," she responded.

"We are calling you about the men that have come to pray over the seats in the arena."

"Yes?" Beth responded," I gave my permission last night."

"Mrs Moore, how many did you clear?"

"I did not give a number, just some local men who are singing in the choir....ah..........probably around 7?" she responded. "How many do we need to give permission."

The security guard responded. "Mrs Moore, we have seven thousand men."

Can you even imagine the blessing that Beth felt when he announced the number of men who had arrived to pray over the seats?

Each chair was important. It is important to God: He provided those men.

I am still forever in awe of that many men, on a work day, showed up to pray for women.

How important is your seat when you sit before the Lord? Do you plan your time to worship Him and stick with the plan or is there interference?

We discovered when we studied the desk that our notebook should reflect a planned time to sit before the Lord and study His word. Evaluate your discipline to honor that time with the Lord.

Do you have a set time of day?
Do you need to make one?
Do you stick to your time of day?
Do you sacrifice more time periodically?

A chair says that I want you to sit down. This woman had prepared a place for Elisha to get off his feet. Do not underestimate its place in the room. It's place is making room for God to come into your life.

The below scripture event occurs in the house of a Pharisee, a religious figure in the ancient world. Invited guests were at the main table while others were along the outside wall of the room, listening to the conversation.

Luke 7:36 says...."Jesus went to the Pharisee's house, and sat down to eat. 37) And behold, a woman in the city who was a sinner, when she knew that Jesus sat at the table in the Pharisee's house, brought an alabaster flask of fragrant oil, 38) and stood at His feet behind Him weeping; and she began to wash His feet with her tears, and wiped them with the hair of her head; and she kissed His feet and anointed them with the fragrant oil."

This story is a beautiful one that shows humility and devotion to Christ. To bathe His feet with her tears, to wipe His feet with her hair and kiss His feet must have fulfilled her. She shows courage to enter this home and give this service in front of a crowd of people that knew her as a sinner.

According to the scripture, does she speak?_____1)

What do her actions say?

Her anointing of Jesus was in response to His message of compassion for sinners.

Some people **sit** in darkness:

Luke 1:79 "To give light to those who sit in darkness and the shadow of death."

We know that the Messiah provided the light of truth and forgiveness to those blinded by the darkness of their sins. This scripture is Zaharias prophesies of John's ministry.

Do you know people who sit in darkness, that need our prayers and need to see Jesus in our lives?

Be consciously aware of those who sit in darkness. Make it a habit to pray for them in a significant way. Do the things below to remember those who you want to pray for on a consistent basis:

Every time you turn the lights out in a room you will pray for:

Each time you turn the lights on in a room you pray for:

Prayer: Thank you Jesus for coming into our lives to establish Your Kingdom. Let us worship You. Jesus, let us humbly bow at your feet in devotion to You, asking for forgiveness of sin and allowing us to become Your light in this dark world.

ANSWER:

No

The Chair God sits

WEEK 5 DAY 3

The Shunammite woman has prepared for Elisha a chair for his room.

Her preparation is more than a simple chair. It provides the prophet Elisha a place to rest and study and eat.

Pull up a seat. Get a cup of coffee because there is a lot of scripture today. We will look at some other seats in the Bible.

Moses' Seat:

Worship in the synagogue in Jesus' day began with the recitation of the Shema. The Shema, are the Hebrew words in the passage in Deut 6:4–9"

> Hear, O Israel:
> The Lord our God,
> The Lord is one!
> You shall love the Lord your God
> with all your heart,
> with all your soul, and
> with all your strength.
>
> And these words which I command you today
> shall be in your heart.
> You shall teach them diligently to your children, and
> shall talk of them
> when you sit in your house,
> when you walk by the way,
> when you lie down and
> when you rise up.
> You shall bind them as a sign on your hand, and they shall be as frontlets
> between your eyes.
> You shall write them on your doorposts of your house and on your gates.

The Hebrew Program of Service

The Shema (above)
Prayer
Congregation: Amen

Lesson from the Law of Moses
    (Interpreter translated into Aramic,
    verse by verse words from
    the Law of Moses)

Passage from the Prophets***
    (Interpreter translated the Passage from the Prophets)

Sermon
    (the speaker sat down – Luke 4:20)

Benediction

Congregation: Amen

The Shema is read. These are the words above from Deut. 6:4-9. This is the greatest command in the words of God to love the Lord.

Shema means HEAR. Deut. 6:4-9 is called The Shema because it is this verse which is the celebrated basic confession of faith in Judaism.

Read Deut.4:6-9 above– again– and say in your own words what they mean to you, for these are the greatest command from God.

Next is the prayer: The congregation would stand toward Jerusalem with hands extended. The people would say "Amen" at the close of the prayer.

Luke, the Doctor, tells the story of Jesus' rejection in Nazareth in Luke 4. Jesus was given the scripture to read the Passage from the Prophets***.

Note: The above program list where Jesus would read the passage.

This reading is seen in Luke 4:16–22:

"So He came to Nazareth, where He had been brought up. And as His custom was, He went into the synagogue on the Sabbath day, and stood up to read. And He was handed the book of the Prophet Isaiah. And when He had opened the book, He found the place where it was written.

> "The Spirit of the Lord is upon Me,
> Because He has anointed Me,
> To preach the gospel to the poor;
> He has sent Me to heal the brokenhearted.
> To proclaim liberty to the captives
> And recovery of sight to the blind,
> To set at liberty those who are oppressed;
> To proclaim the acceptable year of the Lord."

Then Jesus closed the book, and gave it back to the attendant and sat down. And the eyes of all who were in the synagogue were fixed on Him. And He began to say to them, "Today this Scripture is fulfilled in your hearing." So all bore witness to Him, and marveled at the gracious words which proceeded out of His mouth.

Jesus spoke in the Hebrew program when the prophetic word was read. This passage comes from the prophet Isaiah in Isaiah 61, the passage of the Prophet.

Quoting scripture Luke 4:17: "And He was handed the book of the prophet Isaiah. And when He had opened the book, He found the place where it was written."

By citing Isaiah 61, Jesus was claiming to be a royal figure and to have a prophetic mission.

He closed the book in the middle of the sentence because the next phrase, "the day of vengeance of our God", had not yet been fulfilled.

Who handed Him the book and who did He hand it back to after the reading?_____ _____1)

What did He do after He finished the reading?_____2)

The synagogues had an official chair called Moses' seat.

Note that Jesus sat in this seat after He read....
Matt 23:2 Jesus addresses this seat.

"Jesus spoke. 'The scribe and the Pharisees sit in Moses' seat.'"

What did He say to them?_____3)

Match what Jesus came to do:

_____the gospel to the poor	Heal
_____the brokenhearted	Set liberty
_____to the captives	Proclaim
_____of sight to the blind	Preach
_____to those who are oppressed	Recovery
_____the acceptable year of the Lord.	Liberty

Jesus came to preach, to heal, give liberty, recovery, to set, to proclaim.

Who did He heal? _____4)

Referring to those who were discouraged because of their plight in life.

Are you brokenhearted?

If this is who you are, Jesus came to heal you so that you can become His son or daughter, a child of God.

To whom does He give liberty?_____ (5)

The Israelites were in exile in the Old Testament.

In the New Testament captivity is sin. Jesus heals us from sin. Even if we ask forgiveness over and over, Jesus forgives. He can set us free from sin. If you are captive, Jesus came to free you so that you can become free in Him. Therefore, you become sinless. You become the sons and daughters of God.

Jesus came to free us from sin and He has the power to do so.

Scripture proclaims Christ's forgiveness of sin and His power to forgive:

Luke 1:77 "To give knowledge of salvation to His people by the remission of their sins,"

Luke 7:47 "Therefore, I say to you, her sins, which are many, are forgiven, for she loved much. But to whom little is forgiven, the same loves little."

Luke 24:47 "That repentance and remission of sins should be preached in His name to all nations, beginning at Jerusalem."
The greatest sin is not accepting Christ as Lord.

Acts 2:38 "Then Peter said to them, 'Repent, and let every one of you be baptized in the name of Jesus Christ for the remission of sins; and you shall receive the gift of the Holy Spirit.'"

Acts 5:31 "Him God has exalted to His right hand to be Prince and Savior, to give repentance to Israel and forgiveness of sins."

Acts 10:43 "To Him all the prophets witness that, through His name, whoever believes in Him will receive remission of sins."

Acts 13:38 "Therefore let it be known to you, brethren, that through this Man is preached to you the forgiveness of sins;"

Acts 26:18 "To open their eyes, in order to turn them from darkness to light, and from the power of Satan to God, that they receive forgiveness of sins and an inheritance among those who are sanctified by faith in Me."

~Are you in need of a miracle?

Jesus gives **sight** to the blind. There are two types of blindness in this reference:

Physical: not seeing; blind

Luke 7:22 "Jesus answered and said to them, 'Go and tell John the things you have seen and heard: that the blind see, the lame walk, the lepers are cleansed, the deaf hear, the dead are raised, the poor have the gospel preached to them.'"

Spiritual: Not seeing that Christ is the Messiah:

Luke 1:78-79 "Through the tender mercy of our God, with which the Dayspring from on high has visited us; To give light to those who sit in darkness and the shadow of death."

Luke 10:23-24 "Then He turned to His disciples and said privately, 'Blessed are the eyes which see the things you see, for I tell you that many prophets and kings have desired to see what you see, and have not seen it, and to hear what you hear, and have not heard it.'"

Luke 18:41-43 "Jesus asked him. 'What do you want Me to do for you?' He said, 'Lord, that I may receive my sight.' Then Jesus said to him, 'Receive your sight; Your faith has made you well.' And immediately he received his sight, and followed Him, glorifying God. And all the people, when they saw it, gave praise to God."

~Jesus proclaims **the acceptable year of the Lord.** Every fiftieth year all debt was forgiven. Slaves were given their freedom and ancestral land was given back to its original family. A new start was the Year of Jubilee.

Do you need a new start?

Jesus offers a total cancellation of spiritual debt and a new beginning to those who respond to His message.

The Davidic Throne

The Davidic throne (Rev. 3:21) "In that kingdom the twelve apostles will sit on twelve thrones judging the twelve tribes of Israel."

God chose David to be king, of Israel. The Israelites chose Saul as the first king but David was the chosen king by God. In Isaiah's prophecy of the King of Kings, the government of the promised Son, Isaiah says in Is.9:7

> "Of the increase of His government and peace
> There will be no end.
> Upon the throne of David and over His kingdom..."

Are these words familiar?____ They are the ones read during the Christmas season about the prophecy of Jesus, the Messiah to come.

This King, this coming Child, will occupy the throne of David. This King forever fulfills God's promise to David. The Davidic covenant is established in 2 Samuel 7:8. Listen to the words to see the symbolism of Christ.

"Now therefore, thus says the Lord of hosts: 'I took you from the sheepfold, from following the sheep, to be ruler over My people, over Israel. And I have been with you wherever you have gone, and have cut off all your enemies from before you, and have made you a great name, like the name of the great men who are on the earth. Moreover I will appoint a place for My people Israel, and will plant them, that they may dwell in a place of their own and move no more; nor shall the sons of wickedness oppress them anymore, as previously, since the time that I commanded judges to be over My people Israel, and have caused you to rest from all your enemies. Also the Lord tells you He will make you a house.

When your days are fulfilled and you rest with your fathers, I will set up your seed after you, who will come from your body, and I will establish his kingdom. He shall build a house for My name, and I will establish the throne of his kingdom forever. I will be his Father, and he shall be My son. If he commits iniquity, I will chasten him with the rod of men and with the blows of the sons of men. But My mercy shall not depart from him, as I took it from Saul, whom I removed from before you. And your house and your kingdom shall be established forever before you. **Your throne** shall be established forever." 2 Samuel 7:8

Jesus' throne is forever.

Where does Jesus sit?_____ 6)

Where does God sit?_____ 7)

In Is 40:22 the words are "It is He who sits above the circle of the earth......"

Ps 25:8 "......God sits on His holy throne."

Rev. 4:9 ".....Him who sits on the throne, who lives forever and ever."

Matt 19:28 "Jesus, the Son of Man, sits on the throne of His glory,......"

1 King 22:19 "Then Micah (the prophet) said, "Therefore hear the word of the Lord; I saw the Lord sitting on His throne...."

This is repeated in 2 Chr 18:18 "Then Micah said, ''Therefore hear the word of the Lord. I saw the Lord sitting on His throne…"

Where does the Lord sit? 8)_____

Prayer: Thank you for the promise to us as faithful Christians, that when we overcome as a believers that we will share the actual throne with Christ. Help us to overcome by being like you and following your example by being humbly obedient. Help us to persevere the faith despite the suffering. Amen.

Answers:

1. **The attendant**
2. **He sat down in the Moses Seat**
3. **Spoke and said "Today this scripture is fulfilled"**
4. **The brokenhearted**
5. **The captive**
6. **On His Holy throne**
7. **On the throne**
8. **At the right hand of the throne of the eternal Father**

If you have never seen the words of the Lord speaking of the one who sits on the throne, the appointment of our King, then I wanted to show these words in the scriptures. In 1 Samuel 16:1-13, God instructs Samuel to go to Bethlehem to see Jesse. vs.1

"For I have provided Myself a king among his sons."

Mary and Joseph and the shepherds were all instructed to go to Bethlehem where Christ, the Lord is given.

Luke 2:9-12 "Do not be afraid, for behold, I bring you good tidings of great joy which will be to all people. For there is born in you this day in the city of David (Bethlehem) a Savior, who is Christ the Lord."

Do you see that David, whose name means 'beloved', and Jesus were both in Bethlehem. Both kings were chosen by God to serve as His King.

In 1 Samuel, for the first time in the bible history, Jesse and David are introduced. David is chosen by God that day, through Samuel, to serve as king. They are in the shepherds' fields, in Bethlehem.

Jesse, David's father, the grandson of Ruth and Boaz (Ruth 4:17-22),is also mentioned in the prophesy of Is.11:1,10. Jesse's name means:"MAN" . David's name means "beloved".

David, in Bethlehem and is the beloved son of man, the foreshadow of Jesus, born in Bethlehem, Son of God both are Kings.

David, the first king chosen by God to serve His people.

Christ, the King of kings, serving all mankind.

The Chair– Judgement Seat of Christ

WEEK 5 DAY 4

The Shunammite woman has prepared for Elisha a chair for his room.
Her preparation is more than a simple chair. It provides the Prophet Elisha a place to rest and study and eat.

Yesterday, we looked at the Moses Seat, reading of The Shema and The Davidic Seat.

What does Shema mean:_____1)
What does it proclaim:_____2)

The Davidic Throne is the promise or covenant of the Messiah.

~~~~~~

Today is the second part of the study concerning the chair.
The Judgement Seat of Christ will be covered today. Tomorrow we will finish with the "Great White Throne".

The Judgement Seat of Christ and The Great White Throne are different.
Remember that these two seats are different.
One is for unbelievers and one is for believers.
The Judgement Seat of Christ is for believers.
The Great White Throne is for unbelievers.

The Judgement Seat of Christ is for believers. It is the reward for works after your salvation. Salvation is already established and now all believers stand before Christ to receive their promised rewards.

The Great White Throne seat of judgment is not the same as the Judgment Seat of Christ. This judgement is for non-believers to learn their eternal destiny.

The Judge at both will be Christ but these two events will be separated by 1000 years of time. Do not confuse the two. One is for believers. One is for unbelievers.

These two judgments do bring into focus the two different resurrections mentioned in Revelation. Let's get these two straight.

1st resurrection:
The resurrection unto life-this is The resurrection of the **saved**:
A resurrection of believers in Christ- the saved of God.
Only the saved of God are raised.
These are the ones who will be rewarded for good works

Occurs in 3 stages:

2000 yrs ago- Christ resurrected
Christ arose from the dead is fundamental to our faith
The starting point of our belief system

Future- time of the rapture
All the saved of the church age will be resurrected

Seven years after the rapture-
End of tribulation years
Before the millennium
Tribulation saints resurrected

2nd resurrection 1000 years <u>after</u> the millennium
<u>before</u> eternity begins
aka-resurrection into death

The resurrection of the **unsaved dead** from all ages
Dead from beginning of time till end of time
Dead means physically dead and
living but spiritually dead
They rejected Christ.
Those who follow Satan
(Satan gathers these after he is loosed from the
Abyss at the end of the millennium. These go to
war against God.)

All of these spiritually dead people, from the days of Adam until the end of the millennium, will appear at the great white throne judgment to be sentenced to eternity in the lake of fire.

Christian believers will **NOT** stand before the Great White Throne– that is a judgment reserved for **unbelievers only.**

First Seat in Heaven:

The Judgement Seat of Christ
>We have proclaimed Christ as our Lord. Salvation established.
>Salvation **first. Good works rewarded.
>We will be **rewarded** for good works but not saved by works.

2 Corinthians 5:10 "For we must all appear before the Judgment Seat of Christ, that each one may receive the things done in the body, according to what he has done whether good or bad."

Only believers in Christ appear before the Judgement Seat of Christ. Jesus will determine a believer's faithfulness to Him and reward each person appropriately. It is **not a determination of one's eternal destiny because that issue is decided when a person accepts Christ.

(1 Corinthians 3:11–15) "For no other foundation can anyone lay than that which is laid, which is Jesus Christ. Now if anyone builds on this foundation with gold, silver, precious stones, wood, hay, straw, each one's work will become clear; for the Day will declare it, because it will be revealed by fire; and the fire will test each one's work, of what sort it is. If anyone's work is burned he will suffer loss; but he himself will be saved, yet so as through fire."

Christ will judge the merits of His servants' work, not whether they receive forgiveness of sin. It is the evaluation of believers' works on The Day when Christ will judge the merits of His servants' work.

The risen Christ will preside over this seat and it will occur in Heaven.
Knowing that in the future we will stand before Jesus and face a review of our lives should motivate us to live righteously and faithfully in the present.

Our preparation:

~ **Walk by 3)_____, not by sight.**
~ **Develop a longing for heaven.**
~ **Chief aim in life is to please the _____.4)**
~ **Keep the Judgement Seat of Christ in view.**

The Judgment Seat of Christ– also called the Bema Seat

Christ will judge the spiritually living – the saved
Christ will reject those who have rejected Him & His plan for salvation.

***The Bema Seat is an elevated seat like a throne in the theater at Caesarea on which Herod sat (Acts12:21). It is where the winners of a race went to receive their prize. It means a tribunal, especially of a judge or magistrate. In the New Testament the word is translated judgement seat.

The Judgment Seat of Christ is the first event to happen in heaven after the rapture. We will be given a crown or several crowns depending on life works but clearly we have accepted our Lord as Savior at this judgment.

Crown or Righteousness–	2 Tim 4:8 – Lived righteous
Victor's Crown–	1 Corn 9:25–27 – A crown of self denial
Crown of Life–	James 1:12; Rev. 2:10 – The martyr's crown
Crown or Rejoicing–	1 Thes 2:19 – Soul winners
Crown of Glory–	1 Peter 5:1,4 – Faithful imparters of the Word

Prayer: As we read these words of judgement, let us fine peace that Christ paid the price for our sins and that we will accept Him fully into our lives as the savior of life.

Answers:

1. **HearThe Lord God is One.**
2. **Love the Lord with all your heart, soul and strength.**
3. **Faith**
4. **Father**

The Chair

WEEK 5 DAY 5

Today is our last study day concerning the chair. We looked at Moses Seat and the Davidic Seat. Yesterday we read about the Judgement Seat of Christ and the "Great White Throne".

The Judgement Seat of Christ and the Great White Throne are different. One is for believers and one is for unbelievers.

The great white throne judgment is not the same as the Judgment Seat of Christ. The judge at both will be Christ but these two events will be separated by 1000 years of time. Do not confuse the two.

First Seat in Heaven:
The Judgement Seat of Christ

Second Seat in Heaven– 1000 years after the millennium is over:
The "Great White Throne" of judgment

Rev 20:11-15 "Then I saw a **great white throne** and Him who sat on it, from whose face the earth and the heaven fled away, and there was found no place for them. And I saw the dead small and great, standing before God, and books were opened. And another book was opened, which is the Book of Life. And the dead were judged according to their works, by the things which were written in the books. The sea gave up the dead who were in it, and Death and Hades were cast into the lake of fire. This is the second death. And anyone not found written in the Book of Life was cast into the lake of fire."

The Great White Throne–
    Great– speaks of the One who is the Judge; His awesome power
        This great is _____ 1)
    White–speaks of His divine holiness, purity and righteous justice
        This white is _____ 2)
    Throne–speaks of the One who is worthy to sit on that throne to
        determine the destiny of those who have rejected His death
        on the cross as payment for their sin.

The One who sits is _____ 3)

Where does it take place?   Answer is
–do not know.

It does say that earth and heaven have fled away.

The fleeing away from His presence marks the disappearing of the old universe to make way for the new heaven and the new earth.

2 Peter 3:10 "But the day of the Lord will come as a thief in the night, in which the heavens will pass away with a great noise, and the elements will melt with fervent heat; both the earth and the works that are in it will be burned up."

Peter speaks of Christ second coming when He will judge the unbelievers. No one will hide. Everyone and everything will be exposed or as the verse says "laid bare."

Let's finish that scripture so our hearts will not be upset:

2 Peter 3:11–13 "We ought to live godly lives as we look forward to the day of God and speed its coming. That day will bring about the destruction of the heavens by fire, and the elements will melt in the heat. But in keeping with His promise, we are looking forward to a new heaven and a new earth– the home of righteousness."

Who seats on the "Great White Throne of Judgement"?_____3)

The scripture says "Him". "Him" may be God the Father or both the Father and the Lamb.

1 Cor 15: 24–28 "Then comes **the end**, when He delivers the kingdom to God the Father, when He puts an end to all rule and all authority and power. 25)For He must reign till He has put all enemies under His feet 26)The last enemy that will be destroyed is death. 27) For "He has put all things under His feet." But when He says "all things are put under Him" it is evident that He put all things under Him is excepted. 28) Now when all things are made subject to Him, then the Son Himself will also be subject to Him who put all things under Him, that God may be all in all."

Who sits on the great white throne of judgement is debated between Christ or God. All through Revelation when the throne is mentioned, it is God who is seated referring to the throne of God in heaven. BUT the judge upon the Great White Throne is the Lord Jesus Christ. Jesus speaks in John

John 5:22 "For the Father judges no one, but has committed all judgement to the Son,"

John 5:26 "For as the Father has life in Himself, so He has granted the Son to have life in Himself, 27) and has given Him authority to execute judgment also, because He is the Son of Man."

Acts 10:39-42 "And we are witnesses of all things which He did both in the land of the Jews and in Jerusalem, whom they killed by hanging on a tree. Him God raised up on the third day, and showed Him openly, not to all the people, but to witnesses chosen before by God, even to us who ate and drank with Him after He arose from the dead. And he commanded us to preach to the people, and to testify that it is He who was ordained by God to be Judge of the living and the dead."

**Note:Christ will judge the living and the dead meaning
believers and non-believers.

The end–is referring to all remaining prophetic events that will occur after the rapture of the church and during the climax of history, when Christ puts an end to all rule .

Who puts an end to all rule on earth? _____ 4)

When does this happen? _____ 5)

Christ and the church are joined at Christ's coming. God establishes His kingdom on earth. This time will culminate a new heaven and new earth. All authority and rule will end. God will then subjugate all to Christ, who is Lord over the universe.

Who are the enemies in the 1 Corn.15 scripture? _____ 6)

The last enemy is _____. 7)

The final proof of God's victory and inauguration of the new day of the Lord is God's certain destruction of death.

At this time, after the last enemy death is destroyed, there will be no challenge to the sovereign rule of God over all the universe.

Universal peace and prosperity will rule.

Can I get an Amen?

In the New Jerusalem, both God the Father and God the Son sit on the throne:

Rev. 22:1-3 "And he showed me a pure river of water of life, clear as crystal, proceeding from **the throne of God and of the Lamb.** In the middle of its street, and on either side of the river, was the **tree of life**, which bore twelve fruits, each tree yielding its fruit every month. The leaves of the tree were for the healing of the nations. And there shall be **no more curse**, but the throne of God and of the Lamb shall be in it, and His servants shall serve Him.

Where does the Bible first speak of the "tree of Life?"_____8)

All humanity was excluded from the tree of life after sin entered the world. (Gen. 3:22-24). "Then the Lord God said, 'Behold, the man has become like one of Us, to know good and evil. And now, lest he put out his hand and take also of the tree of life, and eat, and live forever'-23)therefore the Lord God sent him out of the garden of Eden to till the ground from which he was taken. 24) So He drove out the man; and He placed cherubim at the east of the garden of Eden, and a flaming sword which turned every way, to guard the way to the tree of life?"

In Rev.22 the tree is seen on both sides of the river, implying that a new, better and everlasting Eden has come.

What does no more curse mean to you?

God is with us always in our daily walk but the last sentence indicates that we will walk and fellowship with God as Adam and Eve did.

Romans 12:1 "I beseech you therefore, brethren, by the mercies of God that you present your bodies a living sacrifice, holy, acceptable to God, which is your reasonable service. 2) Do not be conformed to this world, but be transformed by the renewing of your mind, that you may prove what is that good and acceptable and perfect will of God."

Rev. 20:4 "And I saw thrones, and they sat on them, and judgment was committed to them. Then I saw the souls of those who had been beheaded for their witness to Jesus and for the word of God, who had not worshiped the beast or his image, and had not received his mark on their hands. And they lived with Christ for a thousand years. But the rest of the dead did not live again until the thousand years were finished."

Recap: These are both judgement on works, but the issue of their acceptance of Christ as the Savior was settled at the time of their earthly and physical death.

The Judgement Seat of Christ ~~~~ Christ is judge
    The **saved** receive degrees of rewards in heaven
The Great White Throne ~~~~~~~~ Christ is judge
    The **unsaved** receive degrees of punishment in hell
    Hell is separation from God.

I do not know who said the following but I have heard many times about the ones that might appear before Christ at the Great White Throne:
    The Devil would just as soon send you to hell from the
    church pew as he would from a bar stool.

No one who appears at the Great White Throne judgment is registered in the Book of Life. Rev. 20:12 "The Book of Life" is opened.

~The Book of Life determines the place of punishment– hell
~The book of deeds determines the degree of his punishment.

Every person in heaven is going to be a **redeemed** sinner.
Every person in hell will be an **unredeemed** sinner.
    No unrepentant person's name will be found in the Book of Life.
    Rev. 20:15 "And anyone not found written in the Book of Life was
        cast into the lake of fire."

Prayer: God our Father, Christ our Savior, as You sit on Your throne, we ask that You forgive us of our sins. We bow down to You and accept You as our personal savior. Lead us not into temptation. Deliver us from evil. Thank you for your word and what it teaches us. Amen.

ANSWERS:

1. **Jesus**
2. **Lord**
3. **Christ**
4. **Christ or God (He)**

5. "When He delivers the kingdom to God the Father, when He puts an end to all rule and all authority and power. 25)For He must reign till He has put all enemies under His feet

    The end of all prophetic events

6. Satan, death

7. death

8. The garden of Eden

The Shunammite Woman
Beth Bonner's story about Light
"This is Who We Are; Becoming the Sons of Man"
Page 91

A story I often convey to help illuminate the truth about God's light is something that occurred to me one day after the sudden death of my beloved sister. Becky was my confidante through out my life.

Praying one morning over a church I pastored, I heard a voice speak in the quietness. It was my sister's voice.
"Rosie, stop striving, just step into the light!"

Totally unexpected, I knew is was Becky who called me Rosie. I was listening for some loud proclamation from heaven or even the phone to ring and for someone on the line to give me a prophetic word from the Lord concerning my situation.

Her voice caught my undivided attention. I felt she was in the room with me. Then I heard her the second time.
"Rosie, don't cry! Step into the light so you can see what to do."

Suddenly from a window there appeared a soft shaft of light. Particles of dust floated down while reflecting the sun's light. I stepped into the light with one foot and it felt good. I walked completely into the shaft of light and I lit up! My skin became an amber color. I felt a radiating warmth over my body. Then a feeling of peace passed in my being which I basked in its warmth. There was no sound. There was nothing.

Closing my eyes, I soaked in the warmth and the peace.
Still no sound. Still nothing. Then in my heart I heard Becky's voice; "Here is your answer. Here in My presence."
I opened my eyes and was stunned by the answer.

The Light! It knows no time, no stoppage except our obstacles we place in its way. The beam of light began to stretch out of my family room and into the foyer. Growing and expanding until it dissipated.

It had not gone, it had infused my heart with peace, knowledge and understanding. The answers to my questions did not come immediately. What I did know is that when I got to a critical point of having to deal with those issues, the Light would reveal truth and grant me the ability to address them in wisdom.

The following Sunday, congregational problems resolved and a presence of peace in our church was experienced which we had never known.

Whether Becky spoke those words or the Holy Spirit used her voice to minister a truth to me, I do not know. I do know that truth was infused to me through her voice which comforted me and gave me peace.

I now allow the Light to reflect and to give a larger space in my life by resigning all worries to The Light. Jesus Christ said, "I am the light of the world." He continues to be that for me- a glorious Light.

The Lampstand

WEEK 6 DAY 1

This week begins our last week of study of The Shunammite Woman. The scripture comes from 2 Kings. The lampstand is the last element that she furnished and prepared for Elisha, the prophet. We will look at all the aspects of the lampstand and end our study this week

Review the scripture:

"Now it happened one day that Elisha went to Shunem, Where there was a notable woman, and she persuaded him to eat some food. So it was, as often as he passed by, he would turn in there to eat some food. (vs.9)And she said to her husband, 'Look now, I know that this is a holy man of God, who passes by us regularly. (vs.10) Please let us make a small upper room on the wall; and let us put a bed for him there, and a table and a chair and a lampstand; so it will be, whenever he comes to us, he can turn in there.'

And it happened one day that he came there, and he turned in to the the upper room and lay down there. Then he said to Gehazi his servant, 'Call this Shunammite woman.' When he had called her, she stood before him. And he said to him, 'Say now to her, 'Look, you have been concerned for us with all this care. What can I do for you? Do you want me to speak on your behalf to the king or to the commander of the army?'

She answered, 'I dwell among my own people.'

So he said, 'What then is to be done for her?'

(vs.14) And Gehazi answered, 'Actually she has no son, and her husband is old.'

So he said, "Call her." When he had called her, she stood in the doorway. Then he said, 'About this time next year you shall embrace a son.'

And she said, 'No, my lord, man of God, do not lie to your maid servant!'

But the woman conceived, and bore a son when the appointed time had come, of which Elisha had told her.

And the child grew. Now it happened one day that he went out to his father, to the reapers. And he said to his father, 'My head, my head!'

So he said to a servant, 'Carry him to his mother.' When he had taken him and brought him to his mother, he sat on her knees till noon, and then died. And she went up and laid him on the bed of the man of God, shut the door upon him, and went out. Then she called to her husband, and said, Please send me one of the young men and one of the donkeys, that I may run to the man of God and come back."

(vs 23) So he said, 'Why are you going to him today? It is neither the New Moon nor the Sabbath.'

And she said, 'It is well.' Then she saddled a donkey, and said to her servant, 'Drive, and go forward; do not slacken the pace for me unless I tell you.' And so she departed, and went to the man of God at Mount Carmel.

So it was, when the man of God saw her afar off, that he said to his servant Gehazi, 'Look, the Shunammite woman!' Please run now to meet her, and say to her, 'Is it well with you? Is it well with your husband? Is it well with the child?'

And she answered, 'It is well.' Now when she came to the man of God at the hill, she caught him by the feet, but Gehazi came near to her to push her away. But the man of God said, 'Let her alone; for her soul is in deep distress, and the Lord has hidden it from me, and has not told me.'

So she said, 'Did I ask a son of my lord? Did I not say, Do not deceive me?'"

Then he said to Gehazi, 'Get yourself ready, and take my staff in your hand, and be on your way. If you meet anyone, do not greet him; and if anyone greets you, do not answer him: but lay my staff on the face of the child.'

And the mother of the child said, 'As the Lord lives, and as your soul lives, I will not leave you.' So he arose and followed her. Now Gehazi went on ahead of them, and laid the staff on the face of the child; but there was neither voice nor hearing. Therefore he went back to meet him, and told him, saying, 'The child has not awakened.'

When Elisha came into the house, there was the child, lying dead on his bed. He went in therefore, shut the door behind the two of them, and prayed to the Lord. And he went up and lay on the child, and put his mouth on his mouth, his eyes on his eyes, and his hands on his hands; and he stretched himself out on the child, and the flesh of the child became warm. He returned and walked back and forth in the house, and again went up and stretched himself out on him; then the child sneezed seven times and the child opened his eyes. And he called Gehazi and said, 'Call this Shunammite woman.' So he called her. And when she came into him, he said. 'Pick up your son.' So she went in, fell at his feet, and bowed to the ground; then she picked up her son and went out."

The Shunammite woman carefully prepares 4 elements in the room for Elisha. What are these elements: 1)

When you type lampstand into your pages on your computer, it appears as a mis-spelled word. In this age we use a lamp stand- not misspelled- A lamp that stands on the floor and is plugged into the wall.

The lampstand of Elisha's old testament days were solid so that the candle holder (the bowl) would catch the candle wax. With no electricity, candles were used to form light. His room was an upper room that would have more light than where the Shunammite woman lived. When evening came light would be needed.

The lampstand was a menorah.

Exodus 25 speaks of the gold lampstand. This lampstand stood in the tabernacle where God would dwell. The gold lampstand is located inside the tabernacle, in the Holy Place, in front of the altar of incense and opposite the table of showbread.

Ex. 25:31- "You shall also make a lampstand of **pure gold**; the lampstand shall be of hammered work. Its shaft, its branches, its bowls, its ornamental knobs, and flowers shall be of **one** piece. 32) And **six** branches shall come out of its sides: **three** branches of the lampstand out of one side and three branches of the lampstand out of the other side. 33) Three bowls shall be made like almond blossoms on one branch, with an ornamental knob and a flower, and three bowls made like almond blossoms on the other branch, with an ornamental knob and a flower----and so for the six branches that come out of the lampstand. 34) On the lampstand itself four bowls shall be made like almond blossoms, each with its ornamental knob and bowl. 35) And there shall be a knob under the first two branches of the same, and a knob under the third two branches that extend from the lampstand. 36) Their knobs and their branches shall be of one piece; all of it shall be one hammered piece of **pure gold.** 37) You shall make **seven** lamps for it, and they shall arrange its lamps so that they give light in front of it. 38) And its wick-trimmers and their trays shall be of pure gold, with all these utensils.

Have you seen a menorah? It is a lovely ornament in the tabernacles.
All the elements are _____ piece. 2)
How many branches?_____ 3) How many on each side?_____ 4)
What type of material was used to make the lampstand?_____ 5)

Lamps were oven baked clay bowls that held pure olive oil. A pinched edge or groove held the wick. But these seven lamps were fashioned with much greater care and precision. They were a magnificent lampstand.

One piece of GOLD. All the elements of the lampstand were to be hammered out of one solid piece of gold. The artist who could do this had to have knowledge and skill in metalwork and an ability in artistry.

How many lamps were there?_____ 6)
In Genesis 1, the number seven means completion. It also means perfection. Judaism uses this same menorah today. The symbolism of the number seven goes back to the creation in Genesis.

How many lamps for it? _____ 7)
How will the light shine? _____ 8)
Do you see other examples of God's love and pleasure in artistry today?

The light in front speaks of the wicks in verse 37. The wicks being on the same side would shed light principally in one direction. The lights would burn at all time, continually, even when no priests were present.

Now turn to Exodus 37:17 –24

"He also made the lampstand of pure gold; of hammered work he made the lampstand. Its shaft, its branches, its bowls, its ornamental knobs, and its flowers were of the same piece. 18)And six branches came out of its sides: three branches of the lampstand out of one side, and three branches of the lampstand out of the other side. 19) There were three bowls made like almond blossoms on one branch, with an ornamental knob and a flower, and three bowls made like almond blossoms on the the other branch, with an ornamental knob and a flower---and so for the six branches coming out of the lampstand. 20) and on the lampstand itself were four bowls made like almond blossoms, each with its ornamental knob and flower. 21) There was a knob under the first two branches of the same, a knob under the first two branches of the same, and a knob under the third two branches of the same, according to the six branches extending from it. 22) Their knobs and their branches were of one piece; all of it was one hammered piece of pure gold. 23)And he made its seven lamps,its wick-trimmers, and its trays of pure gold. 24) Of a talent of pure gold he made it with all its utensils."

Does every detail correspond with the instructions given to Moses?____ 9)
The first verses(Ex. 25) are God's command and speaking to Moses at Mt. Sinai.

What else does God give Moses on Mt Sinai?_____ 10)
Exodus is full of instruction to Moses on Mt. Sinai not just the ten commandments which God wrote on stone for us.

The phrase "written in stone" holds its meaning.

Almond blossoms represent awakening and hope. The petals of the blossom form a cup and several flowers grow next to each other on a single branch.

The second set of verses(Ex.27) are Moses instruction from God to make the lampstand.

God now gives Moses specific instructions on the care of the lampstand.

Ex 27:20-21 "And you shall command the children of Israel that they bring you pure oil of pressed olives for the light, to cause the lamp to burn continually. 21) In the tabernacle of meeting, outside the veil which is before the Testimony, Aaron and his sons shall tend it from evening until morning before the Lord. It shall be a statute forever to their generations on behalf of the children of Israel."

Compare the above verse to Lev. 24:1-4 "Then the Lord spoke to Moses saying: 2) Command the **children of Israel** that they bring to you **pure** oil of pressed olives for the light, to make the **lamps burn continually**. 3) Outside the veil of the Testimony, in the tabernacle of meeting. Aaron shall be in charge of it from evening until morning before the Lord continually; it shall be a statute forever in your generations. 4) He shall be in charge of the lamps on the pure gold lampstand before the Lord continually."

Who does God command to bring the oil?_____ **11)**

What type of oil?_____ **of pressed** _____. **12)**

God's standards are high for the fuel for the lamps. Pure oil of pressed olives would be the first oil that the olive oil press would release. This oil is the purest of all pressed. It burns little smoke.

Why should the oil for the lampstand that stood in the tabernacle be pure? 13)

Pressed olives extract pure oil when pounded in a mortar by hand. This produces the finest, lightest olive oil.

The mallet that crushes oil has 4 groves along the handle to press the olive to produce oil for different usages:

First for the purest. It was given to the tabernacle to burn oil.
Second is for purification. Oil was a common medicine to heal.
Third is for eating (or food preparation).
Fourth is for making soaps.

Compare this to how Christ works in us.

First:	He provides us Light. "He is the Light of the world."
Second:	He is the Anointed One."the Lord has anointed Me" Is 61:1
Third:	He provides us nourishment. "I am the bread of life."John 6:48
Fourth:	He cleanses us."He is faithful to cleanse us of all unrighteousness."

1 John 1:9

In Lev 24:2 the lamps are to burn _____. **14)**
The light is perpetual. The first oil, the purest of oil, burns so that it burns continually. Christ is there for us all the time. He gives us light in our darkness.

Matthew 5:15-16, Jesus speaks the Similitudes: 14) "You are the light of the world. A city that is set on a hill cannot be hidden. 15) Nor do they light a lamp and put it under a basket, but on a lampstand, and it gives light to all who are in the house 16) Let your light so shine before men, that they may see your good works and glorify your Father in heaven."

Prayer: Lord, please let us open our hearts that we may be the light that others see that reflects your love. Let us remember that we are the light of the world, to glorify Him to others.

ANSWERS

1. **Bed, desk, chair, lampstand**
2. **One**
3. **Six**
4. **Three**
5. **Pure gold**
6. **Seven**
7. **Seven**
8. **To the front**
9. **Yes**
10. **The ten commandments.**
11. **The children of Israel**
12. **Pure oil of pressed olives**
13. **The lampstand was sacred as well as the tabernacle: to enter the Holy place one must be pure.**
14. **Continually**

The Lampstand

WEEK 6 DAY 2

We began our study of the last element of the Shunammite womans preparation for the prophet Elisha. God gave Moses the instruction for the lampstand in Exodus. The elements of the lampstand were hammered out of one solid piece of gold. The artist who could do this had to have knowledge and skill in metalwork and an ability in artistry. God provided.

Who is this artist, this craftsman that will make this magnificent piece of art?

Lamps were oven baked clay bowls that contained olive oil. A pinched edge or groove held the wick. But these seven lamps would be fashioned with much greater care and precision and placed on a magnificent lampstand.

Ex.31:1-12 "Then the Lord spoke to Moses, saying: 2) 'See, I have called by name **Bezalel** the son of Uri, the son of Hur, of th**e tribe of Judah**. And I have filled him with the Spirit of God, **in wisdom, in understanding, in knowledge and in all manner of workmanship,** to design artistic works, to work in gold, in silver, in bronze, in cutting jewels for setting, in carving wood, and to work in all manner of workmanship.

6) And I, indeed, I have appointed with him Aholiab the son of Ahisamach, of the tribe of Dan and I have put **wisdom in the hearts** of **all the gifted artisans**, that they may make all that I have commanded you: 7) the tabernacle of meeting, the ark of the Testimony and the mercy seat that is on it, and all the furniture of the tabernacle---- 8) the table and its utensils, the pure gold lampstand with all its utensil, the altar of incense, 9) the altar of burnt offering with all its utensils, and the laver and its base--- 10) the garments of ministry, the holy garments for Aaron the priest and the garments of his sons, to minister as priests, 11) and the anointing oil and sweet incense for the holy place. According to all that I have commanded you they shall do.'"

Who is the craftsmen that God has called?_____1)
What tribe is he from? _____2)
What tribe was Jesus from? _____3)
Jesus craft growing up? _____4)

Bezalel's name means "in the shadow of God"

What all did God fill Bezalel with? 5)_____

in _____, **in**_____, **in** _____ **& in all** _____.

He also appointed?_____6)

What did He put in his heart?_____7)

God put wisdom in the heart of others. Who are these?_____8)

We have been given the Holy Spirit. When we accept Christ and are baptized in the Holy Spirit, the Holy Spirit stays with us through everything. In the Old Testament the spirit came and went. But after the resurrection and ascension, Jesus gave us the gift of the Holy Spirit. We must accept the gift of the Holy Spirit.

When we become the sons/daughters of God, we have His Holy Spirit in us all the time. We must accept His Spirit. Notice in verse 2 that God filled him with the Spirit of God. This filling is the work of the Holy Spirit. The Holy Spirit empowered uniquely gifted people to design and build a tabernacle befitting a holy and magnificent God.

In Zechariah 4:2, "And he(the angel) said to me, 'What do you see?'" So I said, 'I am looking, and there is a lampstand of solid gold with a bowl on top of it and on the stand seven lamps with seven pipes to the seven lamps.'"
Seven means– Perfect, Complete and it indicates Fulfillment; Finished.
Here in Zechariah, Joshua tells the angel what he sees.

Revelation 4:5 "And from the throne proceeded lightnings, thunderings, and voices. Seven lamps of fire were burning, which are the **seven Spirits of God.**"

What do you think the lightnings and thunderings represent?

We know that seven means full/ complete. Here the seven lamps or torches present the fullness of the sevenfold character of the Holy Spirit. The seven lamps signify the unique role of the Holy spirit in executing judgment.

The seven spirits of God are seen in Isaiah 11:2–3
"The Spirit of the Lord shall rest upon Him,
The Spirit of wisdom and understanding,
The Spirit of counsel and might,
The Spirit of knowledge and of the fear of the Lord

His delight is in the fear of the Lord, And He shall not judge by the sight of His eyes, Nor decide by the hearing of His ears;"

Look back to the craftsman of the lampstand for the tabernacle, above in Ex.31. **What Spirit did you write that God gave Bezalel, not only for the lampstand but to build the temple:**_____ **9)**

What are the spirits of the Lord: 10)

_____, _____, _____, _____, _____, _____, _____

Notice the words of God in Ex. 31:2-3 "...and I have filled him with the Spirit of God in..."

In Isaiah, David was filled with the power of the Holy Spirit and it is prophecy that the Messiah would be empowered by the Holy Spirit. Jesus was born a man but His power came from the Holy Spirit. We are the sons of God, we possess this same spirit. We are the sons of God.

In Revelation 4:5, John sees in this vision the Holy Spirit in Heaven. The 7 burning lamps represent the Holy Spirit in His fullness and His majesty. Notice that the Seven lamps of fire were burning before the throne. Remember the seven lamps in the tabernacle would burn in front, before the throne.

Ex. 25:37 "You shall make seven lamps for it and they shall arrange its lamps so that they give light in front of it."

In Revelation 1:12 "Then I turned to see the voice that spoke with me. And having turned I saw seven golden lampstands, and in the midst of the seven lampstands One like the Son of Man,...."

The seven golden lampstands represent the **seven churches** and in the midst is Jesus. He stands in the midst of the candle, which the candles have produced. In the midst speaks of love and familiarity.

The lampstands represent the seven _____ **Rev.1:20   11)**
The Seven lamps represent the _____ **Rev.4:5   12)**

The word for lamps in Rev. 4:5 is different from the word for lampstands that symbolize the seven churches in Rev. 1:20. In the first century, lamps were usually made of pottery and burned olive oil through a wick, offering the normal nighttime lighting. In John's vision, the lamps were blazing, more to be seen than to provide light. The work of the Holy Spirit in illuminating the minds of God's people is certainly suggested in this light.

John 14:26: "But the Helper, the Holy Spirit, whom the Father will send in My name, He will teach you all things, and bring to your remembrance all things that I said to you."

Have you heard Him teach you or bring things that Jesus said to your memory?

Was His light, the Holy Spirit, illuminating?

Rev. 5:11–12 "Then I looked, and I heard the voice of many angels around the throne, the living creatures, and the elders; and the number of them was ten thousand times ten thousand, and thousands of thousands, saying with a loud voice: Worthy is the Lamb who was slain
> To receive power, and riches and wisdom,
> And strength and honor and glory and blessing!"

Below listed is the laudatory list of 7 aspects involved in worship of the Lamb compare to attributes of the Lamb and the 7 spirits of God in Isaiah and the Spirit of God given to the craftsmen of the tabernacle which is the spirit of God.

> The attributes of the Lamb named in the angelic host worship. Rev. 5:12
> The angels sing and the elders sing in Revelation. One echoes the other. The first line of their song "Worthy is the Lamb, who was slain," echoes the language of the "Redemption Song from the Elders." The second line is a laudatory list of seven aspects involved in the worship of the Lamb. Rev. 5:11–12
> 7 spirits of God in Isaiah
> The Spirit of God given to the craftsmen of the tabernacle in Ex.

1 Lamb	2 Angel	3 Isaiah	4 Craftsmen
Praise	Power	Wisdom	Wisdom
Glory	Wealth	Understanding	Understanding
Wisdom	Wisdom	Counsel	Knowledge
Thanks	Strength	Might	Might
Honor	Honor	Knowledge	Power
Power	Glory	Honor	Strength
Strength	Praise	Power	Honor

Take different color pencils or crayons or whatever you have and circle or color the same words with same color. Ex: The word Power in blue; Wisdom in Green.

Quick Note: In making reference within the Holman commentary, I was glancing through the study of Revelation. The references I used were all dog eared prior to my reading. I had to stop in awe that the Holy Spirit not only brought to my memory but nicely marked for me. Holy is the God our Father, the Helper was there for me.

From my favorite spiritual writer in Disciplines of A Beautiful Woman:

> The light of God surrounds me;
> The love of God enfolds me;
> The power of God protects me;
> The presence of God watches over me;
> Where ever I am, God is.
>
> Anne Ortlund

"Remember, friend, where your real living is going on....in your thinking, in your reacting, in your heart of hearts---here is where your walk with God begins and continues. So when you start to move into trusting Him, stay there. Do not wander out into worry and doubt." Anne Ortlund

Pray: For knowledge and awareness that you have the Spirit of God within You!

Answers:

1. **Bezalel**
2. **The tribe of Judah**
3. **The tribe of Judah**
4. **Carpenter**
5. **Spirit of God**
   in wisdom
   in knowledge
   in understanding
   in all manner of workmanship

6. **Aholiab**
7. **Wisdom**

8. **All the gifted artisan**
9. **The Spirit of God**
   Reflect the awesome majesty of God/recall the divine authority to   judge
10. **Wisdom, knowledge, understanding workmanship**
    Wisdom, understanding, counsel, might, knowledge,
    fear of the Lord,   judgement
11. **Churches**
12. **Spirit of God.**

1	2	3	4)
Praise	Power	Wisdom	Wisdom
Glory	Wealth	Understanding	Understanding
Wisdom	Wisdom	Counsel	Knowledge
Thanks	Strength	Might	Might
Honor	Honor	Knowledge	Power
Power	Glory	Honor	Strength
Strength	Praise	Power	Honor

All have
   Honor
   Power
   Wisdom

Strength is in 3 while might is also with strength and Might

Knowledge is in 2– The same as Understanding

Praise and Glory are seen in 2

Counsel is in only 1– Spirits of God

Wealth is in only 1– Spirits of God

Thanks is in only 1 – Attributes of the lamb in the angelic host

The Lampstand and The Light

WEEK 6 DAY 3

Whenever light is being addressed in God's contexts, it is usually referring to a form of guidance. Jesus is the light of the world. He shines and illuminates from within us. When we allow Him to be in us, not only will our paths be clear, but wherever we go manifesting His light, the residual effect will cause others to see what truly surrounds them.

What is your definition of light?

The absence of light is darkness. As dark grows darker the light will grow brighter. In the darkest of hours, any form of light seems so much brighter as it pops out of the dark background. Our world has darken but the sons of God begin to shine brighter and brighter. The darkness grows with speed and intensity and the lightness gets brighter.

Have you seen the world getting darker and the light getting brighter? When you look at the stars in the sky what do you see?

Jesus came to give light to the world. He walked on this earth beside the disciples and many others. After His resurrection and ascension, He sent the Holy Spirit to live within us. Jesus walked beside them, but now He lives within us.

The Spirit of the Lord God is in us and we shine His light. Look at Isaiah 60:19–

"The sun shall no longer be your light by day,
nor for brightness shall the moon give light to you;
But the Lord will be to you an everlasting light, And your God your glory.
Your sun shall no longer go down,
For the Lord will be your everlasting light,
And the days of your mourning shall be ended.
Also your people shall all be righteous;
The shall inherit the land forever,

The branch of My planting,
The work of My hands,
That I may be glorified.
A little one shall become a thousand,
And a small one a strong nation.
I, the Lord will hasten it in its time."

Our growing in years decreases our close up vision. We can only see as far as the light allows. When our light grows dim, our vision is impaired. This concept relates to the light that shines within us. If we walk away from the practice of communing with our Lord Jesus Christ, then our light begins to dim. He is still there. He will never leave us, but we must participate in a growing relationship with Him.

How are you growing in your relationship with Jesus?

We can never blame God for an encounter of confusion or doubt or insecurity. This condition is the result of something being out of the scope of His illumination. Be aware of these things:

God never burns out....My Father is at work all the time.
The light of His glory never diminishes.

How do you seek His light to shine within you?

Write from memory scriptures that contain the word light, scripture that light up your life when you think of them. You can also use songs:

Tomorrow will be full of scripture that gives us light. Look at the stars before you go to bed tonight. Be aware of how much God loves you in His large universe.

Prayer: Dear Lord, You shine so brightly. Your light gives us hope in this dark world. I love you Lord for allowing your light to shine within me so bright that others see. Thank you for giving me your warmth. Amen.

The Lampstand and The Light

WEEK 6 DAY 4

Today we will use His Word to understand more about light.

The scripture is written, but feel free to use your version of the Bible for better understanding.

Gen. 1:3 and 5
"Then God said, Let there be light: ....God called the light Day."
Where is the light: _____ 1)
Who named the light:_____ 2)
In vs.5; God calls the light good... "it was good."

"Your word is a lamp to my feet and a light to my path."Ps 119:105
Where is the light? _____ 3)

"The Lord is my light and my salvation: Whom shall I fear?" Ps 27:1
Where is the light? _____ 4)

"The poor man and the oppressor have this in common: The Lord gives light to the eyes of both." Prov 29:13
Who does God give His light to?_____ 5)

Jesus attested that God causes rain to fall on the just and the unjust in Matt. 5:45.

"Truly the light is sweet, And it is pleasant for the eyes to behold the sun;" Ecc.11:7 **Where is the light?** _____ 6)

Can you recall a time when walking into the light of the sun?
How did you feel?
Do you believe you can feel the same penetration of light with Christ?

"O house of Jacob, come and let us walk in the light of the Lord." Is 2:5
Where is the light?_____7)

Light here is used as a metaphor for God's law which illuminates the path that leads to everlasting life. That is old testament, but now we have Christ light that lives within us. We walk in the light of the Lord.

"To the law and to the testimony! If they do not speak according to this word, it is because there is no light in them." Is 8:20
Where is the light?_____8)

"I will bring the blind by a way they did not know; I will lead them in paths they have not known. I will make darkness light before them, and crooked places straight. These things I will do for them." Is. 42:16
Where is the light?_____9)

"Then your light shall break forth like the morning, Your healing shall spring forth speedily, And your righteousness shall go before you. The glory of the Lord shall be your rear guard." Is. 58:8
Where is the Light?_____10)

"Arise, shine; For your light has come! And the glory of the Lord is risen upon you. For behold, the darkness shall cover the earth, And deep darkness the people; But the Lord will arise over you, And His glory will be seen upon you. The Gentiles shall come to your light, And kings to the brightness of your rising." Is. 60:1–6
Where is the light?_____11)

"Your sun shall no longer go down, Nor shall your moon withdraw itself; For the Lord will be your everlasting light, And the day of your mourning shall be ended." Is 60:20
Who is the light?_____12)

The people who sat in darkness have seen a great light, And upon those who sat in the region and shadow of death Light has dawned." Matt.4:16

Who are the people who sat in darkness?_____13)

Who is the Light?_____14)

"Let your light so shine before men, that they may see your good works and glorify you Father in heaven." Matt. 5:16
Where is the light?_____ 15)

"So the master commended the unjust steward because he had dealt shrewdly. For the sons of this world are more shrewd in their generation than the sons of light." Luke 16:8
Who are the sons of light?_____ 16)

"In Him was life, and the life was the light of men. And the light shines in the darkness and the darkness did not comprehend it." John 1:4
Where is the light? _____ 17)
Who is the darkness and why do they not comprehend?_____ 18)

"Then Jesus spoke to them again, saying, 'I am the light of the world. He who follows Me shall **not** walk in darkness, but have the light of life.'" John 8:12
Who is the light?_____ 19)

"That was the true Light which gives light to every man coming into the world."John 1:9 **Who is the Light?**_____ 20)

And then we become the sons of God by His light:

"But as many as received Him, to them He gave the right to become children of God, to those who believe in His name: who were born, not of blood, nor of the will of the flesh, nor of the will of man, but of God." John 1:12,13
Who receive the light?_____ 21)

"For you were once darkness, but now you are light in the Lord. Walk as children of light." Eph 5:8 **Who is the light?**_____ 22)

"Awake, you who sleep, Arise from the dead, And Christ will give you light."
Eph 5:14 **Who gives the light?**_____ 23)

"You are all sons of light and sons of the day. We are not of the night nor of darkness." 1 Thes 5:5
Who is the light?_____ 24)

"The city had no need of the sun or of the moon to shine in it, for the glory of God illuminated it. The Lamb is its light." Rev 21:23
Who is the light?_____ 25)

"There shall be no light there: They need no lamp nor light of the sun, for the Lord God gives them light. And they shall reign forever and ever." Rev.22:5
Who is the light?_____26)

Stay in His Light by practicing His Love. We will have honest doubts, hopes and fears. Christ purposed to disrobe Himself of His divine dignity and descend to our sinful planet because we, His sons and daughters, have eternity in our hearts.

Thus, we bear God's image, His light.
Only in Jesus, in the Light, can ultimate satisfaction, wisdom, and joy be found.

God reveals Himself more to us as we grow closer to Him. When His light is revealed, we then become a reflector of Him. His peace resides in us. We become His sons and daughters.

In Angela Thomas' study, **Stronger**, page 28, Angela writes:

"In Luke 15, the father watched as his prodigal son chose to take his inheritance and move to a distant country. While his son was away squandering his life, the father never stopped loving him, but apart from his father, the son suffered all the consequences of his sin and his choices. Only when the prodigal returned did he encounter the grace of his father for his mistakes."

"For you were straying like sheep, but have now returned to the Shepherd and Overseer of your souls." 1 Peter 2:25

It is "A peace that passes all understanding."
You shall be led forth with peace. Jesus is the Light of the world.

Prayer: Dear Father, Thank you for Jesus. Thank you for His Light so bright that it shines within us. Thank you for Your Everlasting Peace. Amen.

Answers: (Note= answer quickly. Reread and answer if you seem without an answer. My answer may be different than yours. The point is to show you in the scripture that Christ lives in everything and if we are believers in Him then His light will shine through us.)

1. Daylight
2. God
3. To My Path; Everyone who will receive
4. In the Lord
5. The poor man and the oppressor. The Word of God is given to all.
6. In the sun; His creation
7. In the Lord – in God's law
8. To all who receive
9. In Jesus
10. In healing. In righteousness. In the glory of the Lord.
11. The Jesus
12. The Lord
13. Unbelievers
14. In us who know the light–Jesus
15. People–sons and daughters of God– who love and worship Him
16. People who love the Lord – believers
17. Believers in Jesus Christ
18. Non – believers
19. Jesus
20. Jesus
21. The ones who receive Him
22. Jesus
23. Christ
24. Believers
25. The Lamb; Jesus
26. The Lord God

The Lampstand

WEEK 6 DAY 5

The lampstand is in the upper room that the Shunammite woman has prepared. It is a simple piece of furniture that gives much needed light for Elisha during darkness. So true is the Light that Jesus gives to us. His way for us to come to him is simple.

As the light comes forth, so God comes to us.

He **descended** from heaven to come to us.
He **invites** us. He came to us.
He **gives** us the Light.

Think of all the many events that we see in the scripture where an angel appears to give the news of the birth or upcoming event to someone. If the Bible records "Angel of the Lord"; the meaning is Christ. Whether an angel or Angel of the Lord, God speaks to us in many ways including dreams, the scripture and others who belong to Him.

What other events in the Bible stand out to you as God coming down to invite someone to share in God's light— His Glory?

Lets look at scripture about light and see what it references.

Fill in the blanks with the words below that mean light. Choose from these:

Light ~ Deliverance ~ Life ~ True Knowledge ~ Understanding ~Goodness~ Good Fortune~ Goodness ~ Clothing of Honor~ Lifestyle ~ Walking in Character

"In the morning, when it is daylight....: Judges 16:2
"...then he read in front of the Watergate from morning until midday." Neh. 8:3
Light refers to literal or symbolic   .

The Hebrew word often denotes daylight.

"He will redeem his soul from going down to the Pit, that his life shall see the light....that he may be enlightened with the light of life." Job 33:28,30
Light refers to_____

"The Lord is my light and my salvation: Whom shall I fear?" Ps 27:1
Light refers to_____

"For with You is the fountain of Life: In Your light we see light." Ps 36:9
Light refers to _____

"He shall go to the generation of his fathers; they shall never see light."

Ps 49:19
"Do not rejoice over me, my enemy:
   When I fall, I will arise;
   When I sit in darkness,
   The Lord will be a light to me.
   I will bear the indignation of the Lord,
   Because I have sinned against Him,
   Until He pleads my case
   And executes justice for me.
   He will bring me forth to the light;
   I will see His Righteousness." Mic 7:8–9   **Light refers to**_____

"I, the Lord, have called you in righteousness, and will hold your hand; I will keep you and give you as a covenant to the people, as a light to the Gentiles." Isaiah 42:6   **Light refers to** _____

"Indeed He says, 'It is too small a thing that you should be my Servant to raise up the tribes of Jacob, and to restore the preserved ones of Israel; I will also give you as a light to the Gentiles, That you should be My salvation to the ends of the earth.'" Is. 49:6   **Light refers to** _____

"Listen to Me, My people; and give ear to Me, O My nation: For law will proceed from Me, And I will make My justice rest as a light of the peoples." Is.51:4
Light refers to _____

"They grope in the dark without light, And He makes them stagger like a drunken man." Job 12:25   **Light refers to** _____

"But when I looked for good, evil came to me; And when I waited for light, then came darkness." Job 30:26   **Light refers to** _____

"Light is sown for the righteous, And gladness for the upright in heart." PS 97:11   **Light refers to** _____

"Who cover Yourself with lights as with a garment, Who stretch out the heavens like a curtain" Ps. 104:2   **Light refers to** _____

"God came from Teman, The Holy One from Mount Paran. His glory covered the heavens, and the earth was full of His praise. His brightness was like the light; He had rays flashing from His hand, And there His poser was hidden." Hab. 3:3–4   **Light refers to** _____

"O house of Jacob, come and let us walk in the light of the Lord." Is 2:5
Light refers to _____

"Your word is a lamp into my feet and a light to my path." Ps 119:105
Light refers to _____

"But the path of the just is like the shining sun, that shines ever brighter unto the perfect day." Prov 4:18   **Light refers to** _____

"For the commandment is a lamp, and the law a light; Reproofs of instruction are the way of life " Prov.6:23   **Light refers to** _____

The book of John speaks many words about light.

John 1:4 "In Him was life and the life was the **light of men** 5) And **the light shines in the darkness,** and the darkness did not comprehend it." **Light shines in the darkness"**

Christ entered this dark world to give it spiritual light.

Isaiah 9:2 says
"The people who walked in darkness have seen a great light; Those who dwelt in the land of the shadow of death, upon them a light has shined." **Why does the darkness not comprehend it?**

Would you agree that those who do not know Christ do not take hold of who He is or they do not know His power or understand His power?

People who do not believe in Christ resist Him. Have you experienced this resistance when you speak about Christ to a non-believer?

They are resisting because they do not understand.
They resist because they cannot take hold of, they cannot overpower or take control of the situation.
God has the power, not satan.

Jesus is the Life. Jesus is the Light. Those who accept Him are the "sons of light". We see His light in creation, in the beginning. When we receive His light, we become part of the new creation. WE become "sons of God." We become the light.

"I am the light of the world. He who follows Me shall not walk in darkness, but have the light of life."   John 8:12

"Then Jesus said to them, A little while longer the light is with you. Walk while you have the light, lest darkness overtake you: he who walks in darkness does not know where he is going. While you have the light, believe in the light, that you may become sons of light." John 12:35,36

Prayer: Lord, I pray that with the close of this study of the Shunammite woman our eyes have seen your light, accepted your light, and become your children, your sons and daughters. Amen

Answers:

1. Light
2. Deliverance
3. Life
4. Deliverance
5. Knowledge and understanding
6. Knowledge and understanding
7. Knowledge and understanding
8. Knowledge and understanding
9. Good fortune
10. Goodness
11. Clothing of God-honor, majesty, splendor, and glory
12. Clothing of God-honor, majesty, splendor, and glory
13. Character

Luke 6:35 "But love your enemies, do good, and lend, hoping for nothing in return; and your reward will be great, and **you will be sons of the Most High**. 36) For He is kind to the unthankful and evil."

This Is Who You Are

I recently attended a Catholic confirmation and the next week a Methodist confirmation. Both sermons talked about the love we have with in us when we have Jesus Christ and the Holy Spirit. The sermons should have been titled: "Remember Who You Are."

At a recent high school graduation the title of the valedictorian's speech was "This is Who We Are." Her talk focused on enjoying their time now because when she looked back over the 4 years prior tp entering high school the days had gone to quickly.

As our study is titled, "This is Who We Are", we should live with the knowledge of the words written in Romans 12.

Romans 12:1-8 "I beseech you therefore, brethren, by the mercies of God that you present your bodies a living sacrifice, holy, acceptable to God, which is your reasonable service. And do not be conformed by this world, but be transformed by the renewing of your mind, that you may prove what is that good and acceptable and perfect will of God.

For I say, through the grace given to me, to everyone who is among you, not to think of himself more highly than he ought to think, but to think soberly, as God has dealt to each one a measure of faith. For as we have many members in one body, but all the members do not have the same function, so we being many, are one body in Christ, and individually members of one another. Having then gifts differing according to the grace that is given to us, let us use them. If prophecy, let us prophecy in proportion to our faith; or ministry, let us use it in our ministering: he who teaches, in teaching; he who exhorts, in exhortation; he who gives, with liberality; he who leads with diligence; he who shows mercy with cheerfulness.

Let love be without hypocrisy. Abhor what is evil. Cling to what is good. Be kindly affectionate to one another with brotherly love, in honor giving preference to one another; not lagging in diligence, fervent in spirit, serving the Lord; rejoicing in hope, patient in tribulation, continuing steadfastly in prayer; distributing to the needs of the saints in hospitality."

This is who we are:

> We have been called to be different.
> We carry all the family values. Its in our hearts.
> We are Disciples of Jesus Christ
>
> We carry the Holy Spirit....in our hearts.
> We carry God....in our hearts.
>
> We carry Jesus...in our hearts
> We belong to Jesus– you cannot get out of it.

Knowing that we are the sons of God, we should never model our behavior on this world. We wear our relationship with Jesus in our everyday walk with Him. We model Jesus – not the worldly behavior we see in this world.

So stop complaining and do something about it.
Where Jesus wants you to serve....Serve.
Jesus ask us to make hard choices. These will come all our lives.
Remember who you are.
Who are you?

Reference Page

Bonner, Roma Beth, "This Is Who We Are: How We Become The Sons of God".
CreateSpace Independent Publishing Platform, 2014
ISBN-13:978-1496017925 and ISBN-10:1496017927

Ford, Marjorie, "Studies in Revelation". Self Published

Moore, Beth. Living Proof Conference, Knoxville, Tn:Thompson-Boling Arena.
August 10 – 12, 2012

Ortlund, Anne,"Disciplines of the Beautiful Woman"
Publishing Group, 1976
ISBN10-0849929830 and ISBN13- 9780849929830

Ten Boom, Corrie, "The Hiding Place", Bantam Books 1974
ISBN10-0553256696; ISBN13-97809553256697

"The New King James Study Bible", Thomas Nelson, Inc., 1982
Script148148ure taken from New King James Version. Used by permission. All
rights reserved.

"The King James Version of the Holy Bible" Zondervan Publishing House 1977

"The Message Study Bible", NavPress, 2012,
ISBN10-1617478989; ISBN13-978-1617478987

Thomas, Angela,"Stronger", Lifeway Christian Resources, 2013
ISBN10-141587414X; ISBN13-9781415874141

Thank You

Today I sit after many hours of God speaking to me with words to look here and research this scripture or call this person or take a break. With a thankful heart to the many who have inspired me, encouraged me, and made me press forward. I feel God speaking and God's light shining in each one of you.

To my family, Ryan, Penie, Asher, Ava, Ari, Billy, Michelle, Ian, Noah and Clay who tolerated my absence while writing yet encouraged me to continue.

To the Jean Hanger Bible study group who glowed with enthusiasm as I brought the study to them. They continue to enrich my life with energy for the love of God and prayers for me.

To Beth Hall, who laughs with me, while correcting all my mistakes. You are an incredible best friend. Thank you for your tolerance of my ways which are not in any text book except the one authored in my brain.

To Jerald Boyd who corrected my pixels in my pictures (is that right) and never stopped until he had it correct.

To Audrey Sharpe, Char Conner and Whit Middleton, educators, who took the red pencil and marked where corrections should occur while telling me how they feel the Spirit of the Lord in the words. They made me cry while encouraging me.

To Beth Bonner, who tolerated my questions and inspired me with her book. She gave me permission to write this study based on her book. She shares with me her knowledge and also the most beautiful grandchildren.

To DD who arranged time for me to be alone for days so that I could concentrate on the Word of God. Thank you for always being there for me and providing many aspects of making this study come together.

To Dean, my 14 year old poodle, who was my buddy for hours as I studied and wrote; you are the best companion.

I give my highest thanks to God, Jesus and The Holy Spirit, always guiding me in my walk and in the Word.

I thank you, reader of these words, for allowing God to work in your life. What an amazing God we worship.

*Many delays have occurred after the completion of the text and I continued to wonder why God's timing was not as mine. Then after attending the Atlanta Union Mission's Agape Dinner for the homeless, God revealed why He had used the words in the scripture of 2 Kings, of Elisha and the Shunammite Woman.

In 2008, I lived in The Museum Towers across from The Atlanta Union Mission. Every morning at 6 am, I would rise and study the scripture. At 7am the men from the shelter started to walk from the shelter and up the street below my building. I could see each and everyone of these men. They always captured my attention and my prayers. My heart longed for God to protect them, feed them and keep them warm. I prayed for God to reveal to me how I can serve. God touched my heart to give a portion of my income to The Atlanta Union Mission and to cover each individual man that walked in front of me each day in prayer and blessings. I cannot tell you any stories of these men but I know that God filled my heart with their burdens, their joys and their blessings.

My small mind puts the Shunammite woman in the same place where she observed a man with no home visiting Shunem. So she gave her observation to God in prayer. God showed her where to help this visiting prophet to have comfort in his stay in her city. She did not ask for blessings but God gave her many blessings because of her obedience.

Love one another with agape love! No matter your color, your place in society , your poverty or wealth give unconditionally as He guides you and His love will bear witness through you and to you from others.

A portion of the proceeds of The Shunammite Woman will go to the Atlanta Union Mission.

Please write me with comments or to speak at any event or group as the Lord guides you. The video series can be found on You Tube for teaching small groups.
janevanlaar@yahoo.com

Printed in the United States
By Bookmasters